PRAISE FOR
MASTERING THE INSTANT POT

"This pressure cooker enthusiast just learned more about the super powers of the magical machine! Dorsey explains the nuts and bolts succinctly with news-you-can-use detailed cook times and charts. The stuff you may have known is a much-needed refresh, reorienting how to effectively and creatively wield the power of the Instant Pot."

—Melissa Hom, food photographer

"A concise yet thorough education in not only the Instant Pot but the essential fundamentals of cooking itself."

—Brooke Siem, cookbook author
and co-founder of Prohibition Bakery

"This is the perfect Instant Pot book for beginners and everyday users! Jenny does a thorough job of breaking down the different functionalities of the Instant Pot for beginners and home cooks alike. A must-read for anyone with an Instant Pot!"

—Nanette Wong, food photographer

MASTERING THE
INSTANT POT

MASTERING THE
INSTANT POT

A Practical Guide to Using
"The Greatest Kitchen Tool of All Time"

JENNY DORSEY

Good Books®

New York, New York

Good Books books may be purchased in bulk at special
discounts for sales promotion, corporate gifts, fund-raising,
or educational purposes. Special editions can also be created
to specifications. For details, contact the Special Sales
Department, Good Books, 307 West 36th Street, 11th Floor,
New York, NY 10018 or info@skyhorsepublishing.com.

Good Books is an imprint of Skyhorse Publishing, Inc.®, a
Delaware corporation.

Visit our website at www.goodbooks.com.

10 9 8 7 6 5 4 3 2 1

Library of Congress Cataloging-in-Publication Data is
available on file.

Cover design by Qualcom
Cover photograph by Jenny Dorsey

Print ISBN: 978-1-68099-452-0
Ebook ISBN: 978-1-68099-453-7

Printed in China

CONTENTS

INTRODUCTION
TO THE INSTANT POT

What Is the Instant Pot?

The Instant Pot is a brand of tabletop appliance that includes multiple cooking modes, more colloquially known as a *multicooker*. It is the main appliance manufactured and designed by the corporation Double Insight, and it was officially released in 2010. Since its release, the Instant Pot has generated fans worldwide, with tens of thousands of five-star reviews of each model on Amazon—it sold more than 300,000 units in just one day during Amazon's famous "Prime Day" in 2018. The main draw of the Instant Pot is its pressure cooker technology, with its other functionalities offering helpful supporting uses. There are now multiple series within the Instant Pot family, all with slightly different offerings across the product line, which we will go into detail below.

What Are the Different Types of Instant Pots Available?

Name: Max
Sizes: 6 Quart
Price: $200
The most advanced version of the Instant Pot showcases two of its new technological developments: NutriBoost, which creates a boiling motion inside the chamber to extract more nutrients from ingredients such as bones and accurate temperature control within +/- 0.9°F (0.5°C). This allows for sous vide cooking, or cooking foods in plastic or glass while under water at precise temperatures. Another notable feature in the Max is pressure canning, or using the pressure cooker functionality of bringing the chamber temperature above the boiling temperature of water (212° F) to safely destroy bacteria that often grow in foods being preserved for the long term (see more on pressure canning starting on page 92). The full set of features includes Pressure Cook, Pressure Can, Sous Vide, Slow Cook, Rice Cook, Sauté/Brown, Steam, Yogurt Maker, and Warm.

Name: Ultra 10-in-1
Sizes: 3 Quart, 6 Quart, 8 Quart
Prices: $120, $145, $180
This version of the Instant Pot offers the widest variety of functions across its product lines, including Pressure Cook, Slow Cook, Rice Cook, Cake Maker/Egg, Yogurt Maker, Sauté/Brown, Steam, Warm, Sterilize, and Ultra. The most notable addition to this model is the Ultra mode, which offers complete control across all functions for advanced cooks to create custom Instant Pot programs. There is also a useful Altitude Adjustment preset for those living in high altitude climates.

Name: Duo Plus 9-in-1
Sizes: 3 Quart, 6 Quart, 8 Quart
Prices: $100, $130, $160
The latest in Instant Pot's Duo series was officially released in 2017 with the functions Pressure Cook, Rice Cook, Slow Cook, Cake Maker, Yogurt Maker, Steam, Sauté/Brown, and Sterilize. The most notable additions to this model are the Cake Maker specifically for baking, which also doubles as an Egg program for cooking whole eggs, and Sterilize for those interested in pickling, fermenting, and canning at home. Earlier versions of the Duo, titled the Duo 7-in-1, does not include the Sterilize function or Cake Maker setting.

Name: Lux 6-in-1
Sizes: 3 Quart, 6 Quart, 8 Quart
Prices: $60, $80, $110
The most basic version of the Instant Pot originally offered the Pressure Cook, Slow Cook, Rice Cook, Sauté/Brown, Steam, and Warm functions but now also has the Cake Maker setting included.

What Does the Instant Pot Do?

The Instant Pot offers a range of functionalities, from Rice Cook to Yogurt Maker to Sterilize. Its main function, which is present in all models, is the pressure cooker. We will go into further detail on each of its functions in later chapters, but a brief overview and some key examples are below.

Pressure Cook: This is Instant Pot's claim to fame function. In this function, the Instant Pot builds up intense pressure inside its main chamber, which allows any liquid to be heated to a temperature past the standard boiling temperature of 212°F (100°C) and effectively cook food much faster than traditional moist cooking methods like braising or poaching. This typically speeds up cook times by anywhere from 2× to 10×, making it a great way to quickly prepare tough cuts of meat or ingredients like dry beans that would otherwise take many hours to cook. Examples: brisket, beef stew, ham.

Rice Cook: This is a derivative function of the Instant Pot's Pressure Cook function. In the Rice or Multigrain setting, the Instant Pot is cooking the ingredients inside the chamber using its Pressure Cook system, building up pressure to raise the temperature in which water boils past 212° F (100°C) to cook the grains much faster than they ordinarily would in a rice cooker or stovetop.

Slow Cook: In this function, the Instant Pot maintains a steady temperature to cook the components inside the chamber for a long period of time. This will maintain liquid in the final product, such as a soup, and is different from the Pressure Cook function, as there is no pressure inside the chamber, so it can be used for more delicate ingredients such as vegetables or smaller cuts of meat. Examples: lentil soup, eggnog, rice pudding.

Steam: In this function, a small metal insert is placed inside the Instant Pot to prop up ingredients being steamed. Some water is poured into the Instant Pot, and inside, the chamber builds enough pressure to raise the temperature and turn the water into steam to cook the ingredients. This function is particularly useful for delicate vegetables and fish. Examples: steamed broccoli, steamed chicken, steamed fish fillets.

Yogurt Maker: In this function, the Instant Pot follows the temperature cycle needed to make yogurt, or the process of denaturing milk proteins so they thicken and sour in a desirable way. After milk is added to the main chamber, the Instant Pot will raise the temperature to above 180°F. The milk is then cooled, a starter culture added, and then placed back into the Instant Pot to maintain at a steady temperature around 110°F so the "good" bacteria can properly interact with the milk proteins. After a set time of culturing the Instant Pot will stop cooking to avoid unwanted culturing. Examples: Greek yogurt, sour cream, crème fraîche.

Sauté/Browning: In this function, the Instant Pot heats the base of its main chamber—low, medium, or high heat—to allow for a traditional sear, sauté, or brown as would be done on a stovetop. This minimizes the number of pans needed for certain dishes where meats need to be seared prior to the pressure cook or slow cook, or vegetables like onions and garlic need to be sautéed, or spices need to be toasted to release its fragrance. Examples: chicken and mushroom stir fry, minute steak, spiced green beans.

Warm: In this function, the Instant Pot maintains a temperature above the "danger zone," or the temperature zone where bacteria multiplies (40°F–140°F) so that finished food can be enjoyed at a later time without any risks to food safety. This is particularly helpful for pressure cooks or slow cooks made in advance during the day to be served for dinner.

Who Is the Instant Pot For?

The Instant Pot is a versatile appliance that aims to make cooking simpler for everyone. Now that there are three types of Instant Pots with three different sizes, the Instant Pot has a use for almost every household. Because the Instant Pot incorporates the functionality of other appliances, such as a slow cooker, steamer, or rice cooker, it also effectively consolidates space in the kitchen.

In small college dorms or city apartments where the primary cooking is for one or two people, the Instant Pot Mini is a great solution for making staples such as overnight oatmeal, grab-and-go egg bites (just like Starbucks, but freshly made!), healthy mac and cheese, or weeknight chili. It can also be used to bake small cakes, which could be enough of a case to nix the oven altogether.

For couples or small families with greater cooking requirements and a little more space, the Instant Pot 6 Quart is a helpful tool to prepare a meal for four in advance, cooked to order with a delay timer. Possibilities range from braised pork for taco night, spiced chicken curry, brisket sandwiches, to rice pilaf and creamy mashed potatoes or steamed vegetables. It can also be used to lightly pan-fry favorites like pork chop or eggplant parmesan with consistent temperature control.

The largest Instant Pot available, the 8 Quart, makes the most sense for large families, small gatherings, or those interested in serious cooked-and-finished meal prep. It can make an entire pot of mulled wine for a holiday party, a few racks of baby-back ribs for a tailgate, even a turkey for Thanksgiving. Larger versions of popular recipes, such as pulled pork, split pea soup, potato salad, or rice and beans can be made in advance, divvyed up in vacuum-sealed bags and frozen to be eaten later.

Should I Buy the Instant Pot?

Since its release, the Instant Pot has gathered intense momentum from those who love the multicooker and use it regularly. However, it is not an inexpensive appliance and is best suited for those who do plan to cook semi-regularly with its main function, the pressure cooker. Its supporting features, such as the rice cooker, steamer, slow cook, warm, and sauté/brown, are extremely useful but are still functions that can be performed on a regular stovetop and oven.

For beginning cooks and especially those new to the Instant Pot, it is important to be cognizant that there is a learning curve associated with the Instant Pot—or any other multicooker. Learning how quickly and intensely the heating function of each machine works, for example, may take a few tries. Gauging the proper timing of the pressure cooker to tenderize large cuts of meat will take some trial and error. It is worth noting that while the Instant Pot's "cook time" for an item under pressure may be one hour, it still requires some time to build up pressure inside the chamber. Learning these small pieces of how the Instant Pot works is a process but does pay off handsomely (and deliciously!) for those wanting to cook more and create healthier meals at home.

What Will I Learn about the Instant Pot in this Book?

This book will dive into great detail about each of

Instant Pot's standard functions—Pressure Cook, Rice Cook, Yogurt Maker, Slow Cook, Steam, Sauté/Brown and Warm—to give you both a technical explanation of what is happening inside the Instant Pot and common-sense use cases of how to most successfully utilize each of the functions for what you want to cook. While this book does not contain recipes, we will direct you to recipe ideas fantastic meals to make your Instant Pot.

For new users, this book will discuss important safety precautions, basic terminology, and key areas of learning to minimize trial and error. We intend this book as a jumping off point for you to understand the foundational aspects of the Instant Pot and feel well equipped to begin cooking more frequently in the Instant Pot and able to develop your own recipes going forward.

INSTANT POT OPTIONS
ON THE MARKET

There are a variety of Instant Pot alternatives on the market today, better categorized as "multicookers." These machines typically offer anywhere from 3 to 10+ modes, from basic features such as steam, slow cook, and sauté/brown to advanced options such as smoke or sous vide. The main difference between the Instant Pot and other multicookers on the market today is that all generations of Instant Pot models contain a pressure cook mode, whereas other multicookers have wider variation in what is offered.

We have divided the spectrum of available multicookers, including the Instant Pot, along a tiered range from The Basics to The Advanced to compare their differing functionalities. This list is not exhaustive, given the plethora of multicookers, but can be used as a point of reference to best determine what multicooker is best suited for your needs. Depending on your primary use for the Instant Pot modes, you may find one of the three categories suits your home better than others.

The Basics: 5 or fewer functions of standard functionality

Brand: Salton
Size: 5 Liter (5 Quart)
Price: $100
Functions: Pressure Cook, Sauté/Brown, Steam, Slow Cook, Warm

Brand: Aroma
Size: 4 Quart
Price: $110
Functions: Sauté/Brown, Steam, Rice Cook, Steam, Slow Cook, Bake

Brand: Ninja
Size: 6 Quart
Price: $150
Functions: Stove Top, Steam, Slow Cook, Oven

The Classics: Approximately 7 functions of standard functionality

Brand: Crock Pot 8-in-1
Size: 6 Quart
Price: $70
Functions: Slow Cook, Pressure Cook, Sauté/Brown, Steam, Yogurt Maker, Rice Cook

Brand: Fagor LUX
Size: 6 Quart / 8 Quart
Price: $136 / $170
Functions: Pressure Cook, Slow Cook, Rice Cook, Yogurt, Sauté/Brown, Steam, Warm

Brand: Gourmia
Size: 6 Quart
Price: $160
Functions: Pressure Cook, Sauté/Brown, Slow Cook, Rice Cook, Yogurt, Warm, Grill/BBQ, Steam

The Advanced: 10+ functions or contains complex functionality

Brand: Gourmia
Size: 6.5 Quart
Functions: Sous Vide, Sauté/Brown, Bake, Steam, Stew, Roast, Rice Cook, Slow Cook, Yogurt, Warm
Price: $100

Brand: Gourmia
Size: 6.5 Quart
Functions: Hot/Cold Smoke, Pressure Cook, Steam
Price: $260

Price: Wolf Gourmet
Size: 7 Quart
Functions: Sous Vide, Rice Cook, Sauté/Sear, Rice Cook, Slow Cook, Warm
Price: $600

While this book includes Instant Pot in its title, it is by no means exclusively meant only for Instant Pot brand multicookers. In most cases, the Pressure Cook, Rice Cook, Sauté/Brown, Warm, Yogurt Maker, and Steam functions of the Instant Pot are readily comparable to those from other brands, so you will be able to use the tips and tricks in this book to help you navigate multicookers across the spectrum.

FIRST-TIMERS USING THE INSTANT POT

Whether you are a new Instant Pot owner or just looking to brush up on Instant Pot basics, this chapter covers the need-to-know information about using your Instant Pot in the most efficient way. We'll first cover the anatomy of the Instant Pot and how each part works in relation to one another (for cleaning instructions, please reference page 108), walk through the foundational knowledge to start using your Instant Pot effectively, and end with common questions and troubleshooting.

Anatomy of an Instant Pot

The different components of the Instant Pot differ slightly version to version, so on the following pages, we list the pieces present in each model below.

Inner Pot/Inner Chamber

This is the hollow inner chamber of the appliance that holds the ingredients and liquid you are cooking. There will typically be numerical markers to show fill levels with a maximum liquid fill line near the top of the chamber. Instant Pot's inner chambers are made with stainless steel with a copper-clad bottom for efficient heating.

Outer Body/Housing Unit

This is the hollow outer outside of the appliance that holds the inner chamber. On the external cover, you'll find all the buttons with cook modes, presets, and times as well as the display screen on the front. On one side will be the **condensation cup**, which catches any condensation from the lid, and the **scoop shelf**, a little enclave to house the rice scoop the machine comes with. In the back of the machine is the electrical plug. On the inside of the housing unit is the **heating unit**, where heat is applied to the base of the inner chamber to raise the temperature during the cooking process.

Lid

This removable lid clicks into place when attached properly to the outer body. On the inside of the lid, you'll see a **gasket**, or **sealing ring**, made typically of rubber or silicone. This creates an airtight seal between the inner chamber and lid. The sealing ring does retain the smell of food after cooking, so it's helpful to have a second sealing ring if you plan to use the Instant Pot for a variety of differently flavored items or delicate dishes where you don't want any interference. There is also an **anti-block shield**, a contraption that ensures no small pieces of food become lodged in the **pressure release valve**—the valve that allows excess pressure to escape from the Instant Pot—and limit its functionality. Without the anti-block shield, excess pressure could build in the Instant Pot and result in equipment or circuit failure.

The outside of the lid has a **float valve**, or a locking mechanism to prevent the lid from being accidentally opened when there is pressure inside the Instant Pot. Next to the float valve is a **steam release vent** with a steam release handle with two settings: Venting and Sealing. The Venting setting is to release steam from the Instant Pot, such as after the pressure cook is complete, while the Sealing is to contain steam inside the Instant Pot during the pressure cook cycle.

Getting Started with the Instant Pot

Timing

The biggest pain point for new Instant Pot users is properly planning for the full length of time required to cook a specific item in the Instant Pot. Although the item itself may need to only cook 30 minutes, the Instant Pot requires time to adequately build up pressure or heat the inner chamber appropriately—typically at least 5 to 10 minutes. If you are using Pressure Cook with a Natural Pressure Release (see page 29 for details), factor in another 10 to 15 minutes once the cook time has completed. Overall, a general rule of thumb is to add 20 to 30 minutes of time when planning to cook with the Instant Pot.

The Instant Pot also comes with a Delay Timer program, where you can set the Instant Pot to start the cook cycle at a later time. This is perfect for those who want to load ingredients into the Instant Pot and eat a finished meal for lunch or dinner. However, items loaded into the Instant Pot using the Delay Timer are not kept at a refrigerated temperature, thus is limited to food that does not contain eggs, poultry, meat, dairy, seafood, or any other perishable products. For example, the Delay Timer is great for rice, beans, and oats. Alternatively, the Instant Pot features a Keep Warm function that can keep for 10-plus hours, depending on the line of Instant Pot, which may be a perfectly good option to cook during the day and have the finished dish held at a safe temperature for when you arrive back home.

Types of Cooking

The Instant Pot specializes in moist cooking methods, which all require some sort of liquid to activate. Whether the ingredients being cooked are partially or fully sub-merged in the liquid, or not submerged (being steamed), it is important to understand what the Instant Pot can or cannot replace in your kitchen. While the Instant Pot also offers features such as Sauté, because of its moist-cooking forward design, these dry-cooking functional-ities are not an exact replica of traditional methods. For example, the fact the Instant Pot sautés items within a tall-walled chamber does not allow for as free of airflow and evaporation during the sauté process, resulting in a wetter sauté than if the same ingredient was sautéed on the stovetop in a sauté or fry pan.

Safety

Some newcomers to the Instant Pot express concern over the safety of pressure cookers given the press attention around exploding cookers of the past. The Instant Pot has been specially designed with a multitude of fail-safes to ensure even those unfamiliar with the Instant Pot can-not perform anything potentially unsafe with the cooker.

The two main monitors in place are for temperature (if the contents of the inside chamber become too hot or begin to burn, the heating mechanism will turn off) and pressure (excess pressure is released through the pressure release valve during cooking). To avoid any user error, a lid detection system will beep and allow cooking only if the lid has been placed onto the Instant Pot properly, and an anti-block shield prevents any food from clogging the vents of the pressure release valve.

The main safety requirement for Instant Pot users is caution with the escaping steam from the pressure cooker. Steam is hotter than boiling water, so it is important you are extremely careful when releasing the pressure release valve to Venting. The steam typically will escape at an angle, so it is advisable to toggle the valve with a long pair of tongs or other equipment that can serve as an extension of your arm. Alternatively, you can use the Natural Pressure Release option (see page 29) to avoid any steam release at all.

Recipe Conversion

First-timers attempting to use the Instant Pot for recipes previously made in a different appliance will discover the timing on the Instant Pot varies from item to item, recipe to recipe, which can be rather frustrating to start. Generally speaking, the Instant Pot's pressure cooking functionality speeds up the cooking process for most items anywhere from 2× to 10×, usually landing around 4×: a 3-pound whole chicken typically takes 2+ hours to cook in the oven at 400°F but can cook in the Instant Pot in 30 minutes. It will take some trial and error to figure out your favorite recipes in the Instant Pot, but our handy Basic Pressure Cooker Time Chart (page 31) and Basic Rice Cooker Time Chart (page 39) are good places to start your estimates. The Pressure Cook and Rice Cook functionalities both use the process of pressure cooking, so the same increase in speed will be applied for food made in those cook cycles. It's also important to note that when scaling up recipes in the Instant Pot during pressure cooking, you *do not* need to correspondingly increase your cook time—cooking two (3-pound) whole chickens would take the same time as one but require more liquid and take longer for the Instant Pot to build initial pressure.

> When scaling up recipes in the Instant Pot during pressure cooking, you do not need to correspondingly increase your cook time.

The Instant Pot also uses pressure during its Rice Cook and Steam functions, so there will be timing differences between rice cooked in a traditional rice cooker or steamed on the stove versus in the Instant Pot. The approximate timetables of speeding up the cooking process 2× to 10×, with an average of 4×, still hold true here. For steaming, the Instant Pot alleviates any worry over potential evaporation with its airtight seal, allowing you to use less water to steam the same amount of items.

Recipes for Instant Pot's other functions, such as Slow Cook or Sauté, do not differ dramatically in terms of time from its traditional counterparts but the conversion does require some tweaks in cook settings to replicate desired results. Because the Instant Pot heats more evenly than most household stoves and ovens, you can expect more even browning on your finished items. Due to the airtight seal, you may also need to remove some liquid from the recipe so the final dish is not too watery.

Types of Recipes to Get Started

We recommend starting out with basic recipes that will allow you to become comfortable with the different cook functions of the Instant Pot, observe how pressure cooking impacts the final products you are cooking, and get comfortable with how much liquid to use and seasonings/ flavorings to add. Before trying your first recipe, it's helpful to do a test run with just water in the inner chamber to practice working with the pressure release valve—simply add 1 cup of water to the chamber, cook on High Pressure for 2 minutes, then use the Quick Release.

Now that you're comfortable with the basic process, we recommend using the Instant Pot to adapt the following basic recipes you likely already make at home, such as:

- Chicken broth (pressure cook)
- White rice (rice cook)
- Hard boiled eggs (steamer)
- Oatmeal (pressure cook)
- Steamed broccoli (steamer)
- Caramelized onions (sauté)

Common Questions and Troubleshooting

How do I know if my lid is locked?
The lid slides into the Instant Pot's outer body smoothly and will click into place with a sound. You'll notice that the Instant Pot will not allow you to use many cook

programs unless the lid has been properly locked in place.

Can I roast something in my Instant Pot?

The Instant Pot can't exactly replicate the roast of an oven, but you could try pressure cook with minimal amounts of liquid and sear off the ingredient before serving for a relatively similar finish.

What types of cooking can't I do in the Instant Pot?

Most dry-cooking functionalities do not work the same in the Instant Pot, such as bake, roast, toast, or grill. The closest functionality the Instant Pot has for dry cooking is its Sauté program.

Can I fry in the Instant Pot?

It is not advisable to fry in the Instant Pot, as it does not have programs for setting and maintaining oil temperature. Some users will heat oil on the Sauté function, but because the heating does not stop once the oil has reached the optimal temperature, it is easy to burn the food or heat the oil above its smoking point. The Instant Pot also has a relatively deep inner chamber, making it difficult to remove finished fried items from inside.

What types of tools should I use when cooking in the Instant Pot?

The Instant Pot has a metal inner chamber, so it's advisable to use heat-resistant plastic kitchen utensils.

My Instant Pot won't open!

If the Instant Pot will not open easily, that means there is still pressure left inside the chamber that must be released first. Its safety lock ensures users cannot unscrew the lid, preventing huge pillows of hot steam escaping from the Instant Pot mid-cycle or after the cycle when the steam has built up. Make sure the release valve is set to Venting and let all the steam escape until the Instant Pot is silent. The lid will then automatically unlock.

My Instant Pot reads "On" and nothing is happening!
Don't worry! The Instant Pot is still building pressure within the inner chamber. Once it reaches full pressure, it will automatically switch to counting down from the cook time you entered.

PRESSURE COOKER

The Pressure Cook function is the star of the Instant Pot and worth diving into technical detail over so you feel confident in utilizing the full range of its cooking capabilities. To start, we discuss what pressure cooking actually *is* and why it speeds up the cooking process so much, as well as pros and cons of pressure cooking versus more traditional methods like braising or steaming. There are a few specific aspects to the pressure cooker we will explain, such as the Natural Pressure Release or level of pressure. We will then discuss a range of important considerations for pressure cooking different types of foods, such as grains or vegetables or meat, accompanied by a standard time chart for how long certain ingredients without presets should be cooked. Naturally, there is variation and personal preference that changes the time and type of pressure for cooking, but our chart is a good starting point. Finally, we end with common issues and troubleshooting with pressure cooking in the Instant Pot.

What Is Pressure Cooking?

Pressure cooking is the process of cooking food using some amount of liquid inside an appliance with an airtight seal. Because of this seal, the pressure inside the chamber containing the ingredients can amount to what is above the regular atmospheric pressure of the Earth. This allows the liquid inside to boil at a temperature above pure water's standard boiling point of 212°F (100°C) because the resulting steam from water boiling is trapped and cannot evaporate, thus turning back and pushing against the water, causing it to reach a higher boiling temperature. Pressure cookers have set pressure levels, and when that limit is reached, the appliance will automatically let out enough steam and lower its heat source to maintain the proper pressure inside the chamber so the temperature does not continue rising. This additional pressure is typically described in units of pounds per square inch (psi) or, in metric terms, bars; every 1 bar is equal to 15 psi.

The impact of every bar above standard atmospheric pressure is dramatic: at 15 psi, pure water boils at 250°F (121°C). The point of pressure cookers is to minimize the amount of time needed to cook certain ingredients while maintaining the effects of long-term cook methods such as braising. Reducing the amount of time ingredients are subject to high-temperature cooking also retains a higher amount of nutrients in the final dish. The exponential time increase varies ingredient to ingredient, but generally falls in the range of 2× to 10× faster than the traditional method, a good rule of thumb being 4×. Pressure cooking always requires some form of liquid, but works even in instances where the liquid does not submerge the rest of the ingredients because the hot steam—which is the same temperature as the boiling liquid—replaces any original cold air in the chamber and cooks the ingredients.

Important Considerations for Pressure Cooking

The essence of pressure cooking is using some form of liquid as the cooking mechanism. Whether this is water, broth, stock, or sauce, it must contain enough liquid to create the necessary amount of steam to cook the rest of the ingredients. Thus, thick sauces do not fare well in the pressure cooker, as their little amount of liquid quickly evaporates and causes the rest of the ingredients to burn. Conversely, liquid being cooked in the pressure cooker will not thicken despite long periods of cook time because the regular pattern of evaporation does not occur. Thus, a flavorful liquid resulting from cooking pot roast in the pressure cooker, for example, will still be thin and runny and need to be thickened separately after the initial cooking is complete.

The pressure cooker is a fantastic tool for speeding up moist cooking methods, from steaming to braising to poaching. However, its requirement for the presence of liquid (in the form of water or steam) means the "pressure cooker" mode of a multicooker, like the Instant Pot, cannot replace dry cook methods such as searing or grilling. However, most multicookers offer a workaround for this particular drawback by allowing the metal chamber to be heated without the use of the airtight lid. This way, ingredients can be sauted in the inner chamber with similar air circulation as cooking on a stovetop with a tall-walled pot.

One of the key advantages of using a pressure cooker is to speed up the cooking process for many ingredients, especially tougher cuts of meat or grains that would otherwise take hours to cook properly. Our Basic Pressure Cooker Time Chart on page 31 gives average time gauges for various, more commonly found ingredients such as prime rib or potatoes. The times indicated refer to the cook time under pressure, *after* the pressure cooker has already reached the desired pressure level. This usually takes 10 or so minutes, as the heating element must reach a high enough temperature to boil the water and produce enough steam to displace the original cold air and fill the inner chamber. Thus, accurate planning for pressure cooked meals require adding 10 minutes to the cook time for a final process time.

While most of us live in places with slightly different atmospheric pressure, the difference is not dramatic enough to cause significant confusion to our cooking appliances, times, or temperatures. However, for those who live in places of high altitude (over 3,000 feet or 915 meters above sea level), there are issues in pressure cooking that will need to be mitigated. Rather confusingly, higher *elevations* result in lower *atmospheric pressure*, meaning water boils at a *lower* temperature than the standard 212°F (100°C). This causes many boiled foods, such as rice, to be undercooked without the use of a pressure cooker but also results in a variance in cook times for pressure cooking. While the pressure cooker is still able to push the water's boiling point above where it otherwise would land, it is still objectively lower than the standard temperature it would reach—meaning pressure cooker uses in high elevations need to add extra time to all of its pressure cooking recipes. The general rule of thumb is to add 5 percent more time for every 1,000 feet your area is above 2,000 feet above sea level.

What Cooks Best under Pressure?

The best use for the pressure cooker is achieving soft, tender textures from otherwise tough ingredients. Large cuts of meat, especially bone-in cuts, are a perfect item to highlight the pressure cooker's magical capabilities. A 5-pound bone-in pork shoulder may typically take 6+ hours to roast into shreddable, fork-tender meat— but in the Instant Pot, that can be reduced to 2½ hours. Collagen-rich meat cuts, such as tendons and shanks, are also tenderized in the Instant Pot in a way traditional methods are not quite able to replicate due to more intense protein extraction from using a higher boiling temperatures. Hard grains, beans, and legumes are another great case. Beans are often seen as a problematic ingredient, but they can be transformed from completely dry to fully cooked in under an hour *without* soaking.

Because of the effectively zero evaporation during the cook process, much less liquid needs to be used than in traditional moist cooking methods, which helps speed up the cooking process while resulting in an ultra-concentrated final broth. In instances where broth is the final desired dish, especially bone broth, using a pressure cooker extracts much more flavor and nutrients because the high temperature and pressure further breaks down the protein in the meats.

There are ingredients that are not well suited for pressure cooking. Delicate vegetables, such as zucchini, will turn into mush when cooked in the intense conditions of a pressure cooker. Even hardier vegetables like root vegetables—carrots, sweet potatoes—need to be timed carefully in the pressure cooker to avoid turning its texture into baby food despite keeping its original shape. Greens and herbs are excellent flavoring agents in pressure cookers, but turn limp and brown in the chamber—any herbs meant for presentation purposes need to be added after the cooking is complete. Leaner cuts of meat, such as chicken breast or pork tenderloin also are not the best suited for the Instant Pot, as they can overcook quickly. If you are using them, make sure to follow the recipe's cook times carefully.

What's the Difference between Instant Pot's "Low" and "High" Pressure?

The Instant Pot has two pressure settings, a Low and a High. The Low setting operates at 5.8 to 7.2 psi, where water boils at roughly 230°F (110°C). This setting is comparatively less popular than the High setting given the much smaller delta between cook times at Low pressure versus traditional methods. However, it is useful for certain instances where high pressure would damage the structural integrity of the ingredient. Eggs are a great example of an ingredient that uses the Low Pressure setting, as are meatballs and chicken breast.

The High setting operates at 10.2 to 11.6 psi, where water boils at up to 242°F (116°C). This is slightly lower than other brands, which are modeled after the USDA's standard 15 psi. Thus, recipes that have been created for 15 psi machines will need to be adjusted to fit the Instant Pot by adding a few minutes of cook time under pressure. A good rule of thumb is to add 20 percent cooking time for recipes that were created for a 15-psi model of a pressure cooker. Most Instant Pot users will opt for the high pressure option the vast majority of the time.

What Does "Natural Release" versus "Quick Release" mean?

The Natural Pressure Release (NPR) allows the Instant Pot to drop its internal pressure gradually, without excessive steam venting. This is done by turning off the heating mechanism inside the pot, cooling the liquid inside, and letting the chamber depressurize by itself as the liquid stops creating steam. This process generally takes 10 to 15 minutes, during which time the ingredients inside the Instant Pot are still cooking. Thus, it is best to use Natural Pressure Release for ingredients that cannot be over-cooked quickly. However, this is made more complicated by the fact the Natural Pressure Release is better for the texture of many ingredients, such as meats and grains. Rice, for example, is recommended to be processed on Natural Pressure Release only. We have denoted below certain types of ingredients that are generally favorable for Natural Pressure Release, though we recommend experimenting between Natural Pressure Release (NPR) and Quick Release (QR) for all your favorite Instant Pot dishes to see if there is a significant difference.

- Rice, which tends to become mushy or clumpy when released on QR
- Eggs, which are delicate and QR may negatively impact their texture
- Oatmeal, which tends to foam during cooking
- Legumes, which tend to foam during cooking

- High liquid foods (e.g., broth), which tend to sputter upon QR
- High starch foods (e.g., pasta or porridge), which tend to sputter upon QR
- Large cuts of meat, so it can effectively "rest" after cooking during the NPR process

The Quick Release (QR), also known as the Automatic Release, removes the pressure from inside the chamber by forcibly venting the encased steam out of the Instant Pot through a valve in the lid. The position required for the valve to be release steam is clearly labeled Venting. This must be done carefully, as steam and liquids have more heat capacity than air and will burn skin much faster. Compared to the Natural Pressure Release, the Quick Release only takes 1 to 2 minutes but does not cool the Instant Pot in the process, so the chamber is still extremely hot to the touch. However, it does stop the cooking process immediately, making it a better choice for foods that overcook quickly (e.g., lean cuts of meat, seafood, delicate vegetables). It's pertinent to avoid Quick Release when cooking ingredients that tend to foam and froth during the process, as that will escape out the valve and splatter. Overall, the Quick Release is very handy to save time in the holistic cooking process and generally does not negatively impact the final taste of the dish.

When you're using either the NPR or QR, wait for the floating valve to drop completely to indicate all the pressure inside the chamber is gone before twisting to open the lid.

Basic Pressure Cooker Time Chart

Item	Cook Time	High or Low*	NPR or QR
Root vegetables (e.g., butternut squash, sweet potato)	4–6 minutes	High	QR
Hardy vegetables (e.g., broccoli, cabbage)	2–4 minutes	High	QR
Delicate vegetables (e.g., peppers, green beans)	1–3 minutes	High	QR
Chicken, whole, 3–4 lbs	30 minutes	High	NPR
Chicken, breasts	6–8 minutes	High	NPR
Chicken, thighs	8–10 minutes	High	NPR
Pork, lean cuts, boneless	8–10 minutes	High	NPR
Pork, beef, lamb, tough cuts, bone–in, per lb	20–25 minutes	High	NPR
Pork, beef, lamb, stew meat, per lb	10–15 minutes	High	NPR
Pork, beef, boneless roast, per lb	20–25 minutes	High	NPR
Pork, beef, ribs	15–25 minutes	High	NPR
Pork, beef, offals (e.g., pig's feet, oxtail)	60–90 minutes	High	NPR
Lamb leg, boneless	15–20 minutes	High	NPR
Bone broth	60 minutes	High	NPR
Eggs, soft boiled	3 minutes	High	QR
Eggs, hard boiled	5 minutes	High	QR
Beans, dry	40–50 minutes	High	NPR
Beans, soaked	8–15 minutes	High	NPR
Fish, whole	4–5 minutes	High	QR
Fish, fillets	1–3 minutes	High	QR
Shellfish	2–3 minutes	High	QR
Fruits (e.g., apples, pears)	2–4 minutes	High	QR

*Note: You can use the Low setting for all of these, but it will increase the cook time. For example, soft-boiled eggs can be low pressure, 7–8 minutes, QR and hard-boiled eggs can be low pressure, 10–12 minutes, QR.

Common Questions and Troubleshooting

My Instant Pot takes forever to build up enough pressure to start cooking.

The more ingredients you have inside your Instant Pot's chamber, the longer it will take to build pressure. If you frequently cook with frozen items, that may also be part of the reason, as those ingredients slow the speed to boiling for the liquid inside the chamber. The higher the volume and density of the contents within the chamber, the longer it takes for the Instant Pot to build up pressure.

My Instant Pot won't start pressure cooking because it's unable to achieve full pressure.

Make sure your lid's valve is set to Sealing and not Venting, thereby not allowing any steam to escape during the pressurizing process, and also make sure you have not overfilled the inside chamber or added too little liquid—or too thick of a liquid—to the chamber. Remove your lid and check that your sealing ring is intact and not gaping in any areas and that the float valve and anti-block shields are clean. Check the outside bottom of your chamber to ensure it is not dirty and obstructing contact with the heating conduit at the base of the Instant Pot. If your Instant Pot continues to be unable to start pressure cooking, please contact the company directly, as you may have a defective appliance.

What's the minimum amount of water I need to put into my Instant Pot for it to work properly?

Instant Pot's official manual states 1½ cups of liquid, though it depends on the amount of other ingredients in the chamber. It is generally a good idea to have at least

1 cup of liquid in the chamber to help build adequate pressure for cooking, or have about one-third of your ingredients submerged in liquid.

What happens if I fill my Instant Pot above the max fill line?

The max line indicates the amount of liquid the Instant Pot is able to sufficiently heat under a pressurized state. While in most cases a few millimeters over the max line is not enough to cause cooking issues, a significant digression from the max line may result in the Instant Pot being unable to fully pressurize and/or unable to cook the ingredients inside the chamber at the high temperature it could otherwise achieve. This may result in slightly undercooked food, or food that needs to be cooked much longer than usual to achieve the same degree of tenderness.

If I am doubling a recipe, how do I adjust the cooking time in the Instant Pot?

Unlike regular recipe conversions, where you need to adjust cook times and/or water content for larger quantities, the Instant Pot allows you to multiply the quantity of food you're cooking using the same amount of time as the original recipe. Because there is no evaporation in the chamber and the hot steam is maintained consistently once the Instant Pot reaches full pressure, the cook time is predicated on the time it takes for the ingredients to be fully cooked. However, there are instances where recipe amounts are dramatically increased that will require additional cooking time, especially for meats.

Should I steam or pressure cook vegetables and fruits?

It is recommended you steam vegetables and fruits in the Instant Pot instead of pressure cooking to preserve their structural integrity.

How do I cook rice and other grains in the Instant Pot?

Please refer to page 39 for our timetable on cooking rice and other grains.

I followed the Basic Pressure Cooker Time Chart, but my food is under/overcooked.

Our Basic Pressure Cooker Time Chart (page 31) is a starting point of average times to cook different ingredients. It is by no means exhaustive and does not account for the wide range of taste and texture preferences. We recommend you use the chart as a beginning point for your Instant Pot experiments but keep a personalized timetable of pressure settings and cook times for your regular dishes. For those living in high-altitude environments, please note you will need to manually adjust the times in our chart, as they are meant for standard-altitude environments.

Does the Keep Warm feature lengthen the amount of time for Natural Pressure Release?

No, letting your Instant Pot switch to Keep Warm after cooking will not lengthen the amount of time needed for the chamber to de-pressurize. Keep Warm operates between 145°F and 172°F (62°C to 77°C), temperatures which are far below the temperature of the chamber when still pressurized.

RICE COOKER

There is a difference between a traditional, stand-alone rice cooker compared to the Instant Pot —or any multicooker's—Rice Cook function. We will walk through the key differences by first explaining how a basic rice cooker works, how advanced "fuzzy logic" rice cookers build on the basics, and how Instant Pot's Rice Cook is different, what adjustments are needed to cook rice in the Instant Pot, and finally common questions and troubleshooting issues.

How Traditional Rice Cookers Work

In basic rice cookers, thermal sensors measure and control the temperature of the chamber as it heats up the ingredients inside. Once the user fills the chamber with water and rice—usually in a 2 to 1 ratio—the rice cooker heats the water until it boils (212°F or 100°C) and maintains that cooking heat until all the water in the chamber has evaporated—whether turned to steam or absorbed by the rice. Rice cookers are able to sense when the water has evaporated due to the fact water will not rise above its boiling temperature, but dense masses (such as rice, or other grains being cooked) will—thus when the temperature probe senses the ingredients of the chamber reaching temperatures above water's boiling point of 212°F, it will automatically shut off the machine. The main issues users encounter with basic rice cookers are temperature sensor accuracy and sensitivity and inability to adjust the temperature of "doneness" for those living in high-altitude environments where water boils at a lower temperature.

Advanced rice cookers, known colloquially as "fuzzy logic" rice cookers, incorporate an additional level of machine learning to monitor the rice as it cooks and customizes the temperature to deliver more custom and precise results. Instead of the binary options in basic rice cookers (on/off, or rice is cooked/uncooked), fuzzy logic rice cookers are gauging if the specific type of rice being used is cooked the way you intended. For example, brown rice is difficult to cook properly in a basic rice cooker because of its hard exterior (the bran) that has not been removed. While basic rice cookers counteract this with more water—thereby forcing the machine to spend more time cooking the rice—the final rice tends to be mushy in texture. A fuzzy logic rice cooker instead adapts to this coarser grain by automatically lowering the water temperature after boiling and cooking the brown rice longer for a better-cooked final product. Even if the rice added is the same, users can customize the end texture: for sushi rice (a short-grained rice variety more glutinous than other types of rice), a fuzzy logic rice cooker is able to accomplish a firm final product that is just sticky enough. But perhaps most notably, fuzzy logic rice cookers can also correct for human error if the water added is a touch too much or too little by making small changes to the water temperature to ensure the final product is consistent.

How the Instant Pot Cooks Rice

The Instant Pot does not cook rice, or other grains, in its Rice Cook function the same way as either basic *or* advanced rice cookers. Instead, the pre-programmed Rice function acts as a subset of the Pressure Cook function (more details on how pressure cooking works is in the previous chapter). Because of this, the Instant Pot will not automatically detect temperature changes in the rice during the cooking process or use "fuzzy logic" to preempt changes in the chamber due to liquid, steam, or rice doneness. It is also important to realize the Instant Pot's Rice feature is meant specifically for white rice, whereas other grains will need to be manually entered. However, the Instant Pot can cook any variety of rice and grains, and do so much more quickly, efficiently, and well. But because it is using pressure and temperature to cook rice, a few key changes must be made to achieve the same results in the Instant Pot as a traditional rice cooker:

- **Lowering the water-to-rice ratio to 1:1.** The Instant Pot has an extremely tight seal, which means almost no water evaporates during the cooking process. Traditional rice cookers account for evaporation in its suggested water-to-rice ratio, which would yield mushy rice in the Instant Pot. This 1:1 ratio works for all types of rice because while the Instant Pot needs more *time* to fully cook hardier varieties, there is still no evaporation so extra water is not needed.

- **Lowering the time for cooking rice.** Because the Instant Pot uses pressure to cook rice, the final time needed will be considerably shorter than the typical 30 minutes in a rice cooker or stovetop. White rice usually takes only 3 to 8 minutes. Other types of rice, such as brown rice or wild rice, need more time under high pressure—usually 15 to 20 minutes compared to 45 to 60 minutes in a rice cooker or stovetop. There is unfortunately no easy metric or ratio to calculate the decrease of time cooking rice in the Instant Pot versus a rice cooker, so we recommend using our Rice Cook times that follow as the starting point for cooking rice in your Instant Pot.

- **Natural Pressure Release only.** It is important to let your Instant Pot release its built up pressure in the rice cooking process naturally, versus the Quick Release. As explained in the previous chapter, in the Natural Pressure Release mode, the ingredients inside the chamber are still cooking very gently. Thus, recipes calling for Natural Pressure Release can be "sped up" by adding cook time and using the Quick Pressure Release upon completion. However, in the case of rice cookery, adding time to the cooking process in order to use Quick Pressure Release frequently results in mushy rice.

Basic Rice Cooker Time Chart

Type of Grain	Water to Rice Ratio	Cook Time	Pressure*
White rice (short grain, medium grain, long grain, basmati)	1:1	3–8 minutes	High
Brown rice (short grain, medium grain, long grain)	1:1	15–20 minutes	High
Wild rice	2:1	20–25 minutes	High
Red rice	2:1	15 minutes	High
Blended rice	2:1	15–20 minutes	High
Sticky rice	1:1	12 minutes	High
Parboiled rice	1.5:1	6 minutes	High
Risotto rice	2–2.5:1	5–7 minutes	High
Quinoa (white, red)	1.5:1	1 minute	High
Grits	1.5:1	10 minutes	High
Farro	2:1	10–15 minutes	High
Bulgur	2:1	10–15 minutes	High
Wheatberry	1.5:1	25–30 minutes	High
Millet	1.75:1	10–15 minutes	High
Cous cous	2:1	2–3 minutes	High
Oats, steel cut	3:1	3–5 minutes	High
Oats, quick cooking	2:1	2–4 minutes	High

*Note: You can use the Low setting, but it will increase cook time, oftentimes by approximately 30 minutes.

Common Questions and Troubleshooting

Should I rinse my rice before cooking?

It depends. Rinsing dry rice helps remove debris and a fine layer of starch that coats each grain. Excess starch in the cooking liquid may cause what many describe as a "gluey" texture in the final cooked rice and the grains to clump together. If you are cooking rice for a dish like a rice pilaf, sushi rice, or fried rice where the ideal is individual rice grains, rinsing is worth the extra time and effort. However, if you are planning to use rice to make a dish like risotto or rice pudding, where a creamy texture is the goal, rinsing the rice before cooking makes achieving this final texture harder and should be avoided.

What about soaking my rice?

Soaking rice serves a very different purpose than rinsing rice. Soaking rice—typically overnight—hydrates the rice grains and begins to break down the proteins in the grains. The former helps the rice cook a little faster, as it has already absorbed some of the water it would otherwise absorb during the cooking process; this reduction in the time of rice being subject to heat leaves more of its natural flavor components (2-acetyl-1-pyrroline) intact and gives the finished product a more aromatic quality. Some will say the cooked rice also has a fluffier texture. Pre-soaking can also help those with gastrointestinal issues digest the cooked rice better.

Should I add salt or oil to my rice?

Neither is necessary, but if you like how cooked rice tastes with salt and/or oil, by all means do so!

When should I add flavoring agents to my rice?

Flavoring agents such as spices or ingredients that need to be cooked (e.g., minced garlic and onions) should be added to the Instant Pot alongside the rice and water to infuse the liquid during the cooking process. Delicate toppings such as fine herbs or ingredients subject to evaporation and/or damage at high temperature, such as vinegar, should be stirred last into the cooked rice.

My rice is still crunchy once cooked.
If your finished rice is slightly wet, but still crunchy, after the cook cycle is complete, it is likely the rice needed more time to absorb the water inside the Instant Pot and reach full hydration. Try again with the same amount of water but add 2 to 3 minutes to your cook time for each cup of dry rice. If your finished rice is completely dry and still al dente, it is likely there was not enough water to fully hydrate the rice. Add 1 to 2 tablespoons of water for every cup of dry rice while keeping the cook time the same.

My rice is mushy once cooked.
If your finished rice is mushy and "gluey," in a somewhat congealed fashion, it is likely there was too much water in the Instant Pot that began to converge the individual rice grains together. Remove 1 to 2 tablespoons of water for every cup of dry rice while keeping the cook time the same. If your finished rice is still in mostly-distinct grains but mushy in texture, it is likely the rice cooked too long and broke down the integrity of the rice grains. Remove 2 to 3 minutes of your cook time for each cup of rice, but keep the water content the same.

YOGURT MAKER

The Instant Pot's Yogurt Maker function mirrors the traditional way of making yogurt on the stovetop but takes the guesswork out of temperature fluctuations in the kitchen. This chapter will walk through the step-by-step instructions of making yogurt, explain what happens at each point of the process, and address common questions and troubleshooting issues.

Yogurt is the lightly thickened, tangy result of milk that has fermented with the right kinds of bacteria to develop lactic acid. The lactic acid decreases the overall pH of the milk, which causes it to form a clotted, gelatinous texture. It also adds that sour taste yogurt is known for and extends the otherwise short shelf-life of the milk. Yogurt has been around for centuries, with more focused research surrounding the food beginning in the 1900s. While different types of bacteria can be used for making yogurt, the Food and Drug Administration (FDA) of the United States mandates that all varieties sold here must contain *Lactobacillus bulgaricus* and *Streptococcus thermophilus*. You can make yogurt at home by purchasing yogurt starter cultures, typically in the form of a powder, or simply buying yogurt from the supermarket to use as your starter. For this book, we have assumed readers are using a store-bought yogurt as their yogurt starter.

The first consideration for making yogurt is what type of milk to use. Yogurt can be made with milk from cows, goats, or sheep—it is worth noting goat milk typically results in a slightly thinner yogurt while sheep milk is a touch sweeter and has more protein, making its yogurt thicker. Whole milk and heavy cream will naturally yield in creamier yogurt over a 2 percent or skim variety. Whichever milk you choose, it's important to select the best quality milk you can find for your yogurt base. These same principles apply to selecting a store-bought plain yogurt as your starter. This store-bought yogurt must be unsweetened, unflavored, and contain active cultures. "Active cultures" will be listed in the ingredients of the yogurt if present.

The Instant Pot will start its Yogurt function by automatically heating your milk above 180°F and beep when complete. This step is important for giving the final yogurt its creamy consistency. You can also heat milk in pre-filled yogurt jars by using the Steam function instead of the Yogurt function. To do this, place yogurt jars filled about 80 percent of the way onto the steamer rack, add water to the base of the Instant Pot, and steam for 2 minutes. Make sure to use Natural Pressure Release to ensure milk does not spout from the vent. Heating the milk is an important step that denatures the milk proteins in a way that will ensure they adhere to each other and form a desirable matrix structure that encapsulates bits of liquid inside versus a runny yogurt with excess liquid on the outside. It is a good idea to double-check the temperature of your milk after heating to confirm it has risen above 180°F. You can skip this step if you are using ultra-pasteurized milk, which is milk that has already been heated to 280°F.

The milk now needs to cool to approximately 110°F, so the temperature is not too hot for the active cultures to begin working (the maximum temperature is 115°F). At this point, you will need to physically remove the metal pot (or yogurt jars) from inside the Instant Pot and either place it into an ice bath or simply cool on the counter. Using a spoon, remove any skins that form, as that will interfere with the final yogurt texture. Once the milk has reached the proper temperature, whisk your store-bought yogurt into the cooled milk and return the metal pot back (or yogurt jars) into the Instant Pot. At this point, the Yogurt function will incubate the bacteria at a steady temperature (roughly 110°F) to let the bacteria work by eating the lactose in the milk and producing lactic acid. The minimum incubation time is 4 hours, with the Instant Pot preset clocking in 8 hours. If desired, adding extra hours to the incubation time typically results in thicker and tangier yogurt.

Common Questions and Troubleshooting

My yogurt fell apart and did not hold shape after incubation.

Your milk most likely did not reach the required 180°F temperature when you first boiled it or because it incubated at too high of a temperature. You can test the temperature of your milk after boiling (or during incubation) with a cooking thermometer to ensure it has reached 180°F or higher.

How can I make my yogurt thicker (but not as thick as Greek-style yogurt)?

Boiling your milk for a longer period of time—5 minutes is enough—will help create a thicker yogurt. You can do this in the Instant Pot be pressing Yogurt and Adjust a second time until Boil appears on the screen. You can also incubate your yogurt for a few hours longer than the Instant Pot preset of 8 hours. You can also use a creamier milk to start the yogurt, such as heavy cream, half-and-half, or whole milk.

How do I make Greek-style yogurt?

Greek-style yogurt with its thicker consistency is made from straining the whey from regular yogurt. After the yogurt is finished incubating in the Instant Pot, pour it into a large strainer lined with cheesecloth and let it drain overnight in the refrigerator. The leftover whey can be used to add a touch of tang to sauces, naturally tenderize meats, or add protein and probiotics to beverages.

Are there milks that do not work well for yogurt-making?

Yes. Lactose-free or lactose-reduced milks unfortunately do not work well for yogurt-making as the bacteria needs to eat sugar (in the form of lactose) to produce lactic acid.

FUNCTION 4

SLOW COOKER

There is some contention in the slow cooker community that the Instant Pot does not adequately perform the duties of a regular slow cooker, alongside many complaints on raw and undercooked meats made using the Instant Pot's Slow Cooker function. This chapter compares and contrasts a traditional slow cooker versus the Instant Pot's version, important adjustments to slow cooker recipes for Instant Pot users when using the Slow Cooker functions, and ends with common questions and troubleshooting.

How Slow Cookers Work

A traditional slow cooker mimics the heating distribution of stovetop cooking, but in a more controlled way, to allow its users to leave something cooking unattended for long periods of time. An inside chamber, typically ceramic or porcelain, wide and short, nests inside the outer body of the slow cooker and is surrounded by a metal heating strip. This heating mechanism controls the temperature of the slow cooker, ensuring it does not rise too far or dip too long during the duration of the cook cycle. The lid, usually made of glass, collects condensation and forms a light seal to the chamber but does not retain pressure. Thus, the inside of a slow cooker maintains the same atmospheric pressure as its surrounding environment, so water boils at the same temperature as it does usually. Some slow cookers also have temperature probes that can be inserted into the main ingredient, as to monitor its internal temperature and slow or stop the heating mechanism when the target temperature is reached. Most slow cookers have three settings: Warm, Low, and High. The temperature range of Low is typically 190°F to 200°F, and High around 212°F, depending on the brand, and advanced versions will allow the user to alternate between the two functions in one cook cycle. The last function, Warm, is usually 145°F to 165°F and meant only for keeping food warm immediately after cooking and is *not* for reheating.

Similar to pressure cookers, slow cookers are a great way to braise tougher and larger cuts of meat or hardier vegetables, make stews and soups, and cook grains. There is more steam loss and evaporation in a slow cooker than a pressure cooker, but less than stovetop cooking, so slow cooker recipes call for their own timetables and slight recipe adjustments—for example, adding less wine than called for in a stovetop recipe, which may be overlooked when transferring to a pressure cooker recipe as the temperature is high enough to burn off the alcohol, but that is not the case for a slow cooker recipe and the alcohol amount should be lowered. Because slow cookers do not employ any type of pressure during the cooking process and use relatively low temperatures, the length of time needed to properly break down the ingredients—connective tissue in meats, starches in vegetables—are much longer than it would be cooking over the stovetop, but yields more consistent and desirable results for certain food preparation styles.

Main Considerations for Using Instant Pot's Slow Cook Function

The Instant Pot's Slow Cook function may technically employ the same principles as traditional slow cooking, but the actual execution of the Slow Cook function is not one-for-one. Two key differences are the shape and materials used for the appliance itself. Although both slow cooker and Instant Pot conducts heat from the bottom of the appliance, slow cookers typically have a metal band that spread this heat evenly alongside the entire chamber's sides *and* the chamber itself is made of ceramic, a material that is known to absorb and retain heat. The chamber of the Instant Pot—and almost all other multicookers—are metal, which does not hold heat in the same way. Although metal works fine in a pressure cooker scenario where the heat is coming both from the bottom and from the top steam, in a slow cooker, the metal pot means there is not as even heat distribution like you would find in a slow cooker. To exacerbate this issue, slow cookers are typically wide and short to accommodate more surface area at the bottom of the cooker adjacent to the heat conductor while Instant Pot chambers are tall and more narrow.

The Instant Pot also has three modes within the Slow Cooker function: Less (190°F to 200°F), Normal (195°F to 205°F), and More (200°F to 210°F) in addition the Keep Warm (145°F to 165°F). While the Less function should hypothetically parallel the Low mode on slow cookers, due to the lowered heat retention of the chamber, the internal temperatures cooking on Less is in actuality much closer to a Keep Warm temperature on a slow cooker. Thus, slow cooker recipes using Low should instead be adjusted for Instant Pot's Normal mode.

> Recipes meant for general slow cookers using Low settings should be adjusted for Instant Pot's Normal mode.

The seal of the Instant Pot during the Slow Cook process is also different from the traditional slow cooker. Some Instant Pot lines may come with a glass lid, while others simply state to switch the pressure release valve to Venting so that steam can escape from the chamber during the cook process. Either way, the amount of evaporation while slow cooking in an Instant Pot is still considerably less than in a slow cooker, which makes for more residual liquid. Thus, slow cooker recipes being made in an Instant Pot on Slow Cook should dial back the liquid to achieve the same final consistency.

Despite its differences, the Instant Pot's Slow Cook function still requires some of the same preparation steps as traditional slow cookers. Because food is being cooked at a very low temperature, some ingredients need extra work to extract desirable flavors. For example, the Maillard reaction—a chemical reaction that typically occurs starting at temperatures above 280°F—is what accounts for the deliciousness of seared steaks or caramelized onions but must be done on a stovetop before transferring ingredients to a slow cooker.

Common Questions and Troubleshooting

What should I use my Slow Cook function for?

The Slow Cook function is particularly useful for hands-off cooking scenarios where you don't want to attend to the Instant Pot during the process. The slow cooker slogan of "set it and forget it" rings true here—in the Slow Cook function, there is no worry that an accidental jiggle may set off the high pressure in the chamber. For those who enjoy prepping food in the morning and having it cook during the work day, the Slow Cook function is a great tool for that process. Since the lid is also not sealed during the Slow Cook process, it's a useful way to cook new foods that you may want to experiment with the flavors or seasonings of during the cook process.

Does slow cooking destroy more nutrients in my food?

Not more so than other cooking methods that require any form of heat. Any type of cooking method is about tradeoffs. For slow cooking, the low temperatures preserve some nutrients that may be cooked away at higher temperatures, but because it cooks for a longer period of time, some nutrients may be cooked away than in methods using shorter cook cycles. Overall, final nutritional content in a slow cooker is not particularly different than other moist heat methods.

Is it safe to cook beans in the slow cooker?

Some beans contain high levels of a toxin known as *phytohaemagglutinin*, which requires high temperatures to be destroyed. Typical slow cook temperatures will not destroy this toxin and thus, make the entire batch of slow cooked food poisonous for human consumption. The most problematic beans in this category are (in order of toxicity): dry red kidney beans, white kidney beans (or cannellini), and broad beans. The best way to cook these beans are to soak them overnight, then boil at 212°F (100°C) for a minimum of 10 minutes—the FDA recommends 30 minutes—before placing them in your slow cooker to continue cooking.

What is the Instant Pot glass lid used for in slow cooking?

The Instant Pot Tempered Glass Lid purposefully offers a loose fit and steam release hole to allow some steam to escape during the cooking process. Some users prefer to use this lid, versus the regular lid set to Venting, during the Slow Cook process, as the amount of steam released is more similar to the traditional slow cook process and allows for easy flavor adjustments throughout the cook process. The glass lid can also be used for the Steam, Sauté/Brown, and Keep Warm functions, which will be addressed in their own chapters.

STEAMER

The Instant Pot offers two types of steaming: Pressure Steam and Regular Steam. The Pressure Steam uses the setup included in every Instant Pot: a metal trivet that nests inside the inner chamber to either hold an oven-safe glass or stainless steel dish containing the items to be steamed or the items directly on the trivet itself. The Regular Steam requires purchasing an additional glass lid and using the Sauté/Brown, not Steam, function to mimic a traditional steamer. This chapter will compare and contrast these two types of Steam functions against a traditional steamer, important tips on how to set up and use either Steam function properly, a basic timetable for steaming items, and end with common questions and troubleshooting.

How Traditional Steamers Work

There are two main types of steamers available: a stovetop steamer or an electric steamer. Both employ the same technique to deliver the results of steaming, a moist cooking method where food is cooked using hot vapor while inside an enclosed environment. In a stovetop steamer, water (or some type of liquid) is added to a tall-walled pot or wok before a steamer insert filled with the items to be cooked is placed on top of the water. In an electric steamer, water is added to the base chamber of the appliance before single or multiple steamer racks are placed on top. In both instances, the items being steamed are *not* submerged in the water, but held above it, and the water is turned to steam with a direct heat source underneath the pot, whether it be the gas from the range or the electric heating nodule from the appliance. Water boils at 212°F (100°C) and, under no pressure, will turn into steam, which is hotter than water, typically cooking items at around 217°F (103°C). Since the water is evaporating throughout the process of the steaming, stovetop steamers recommend starting with ample amounts of liquid while electric steamers often have a water reservoir that will add water as needed throughout the steam process. In order to keep the hot steam circulating in the steamer and hold the temperature steady, a lid—usually tempered glass—is placed over both the stovetop and electric steamer.

Benefits of Steaming

Steaming is a gentle way to cook foods that also better maintains its nutritional value. Delicate items such as lean proteins, shellfish, and greens benefit the most from steaming as a way to preserve its moisture, color, texture, and flavor. Steam is hotter than water, so steaming also cooks food faster than poaching or boiling, minimizing nutrient loss in the cooking process. Because items being steamed are not in direct contact with water, they are better able to retain nutrients that may otherwise seep out during the cooking process. Fruit is another popular food group for steaming, as the quick but gentle cooking holds onto the maximum flavor and vitamins. Certain sweets and pastries also use steaming instead of baking, such as steamed buns or steamed custards, to create a uniquely soft texture in the final product often moister than baking with a bain-marie.

How to Use the Regular Steam Function

The Regular Steam function on the Instant Pot works the same as a traditional steamer. A steamer insert, whether it is the metal trivet included with the Instant Pot or a standing basket-type insert purchased separately, is placed into the Instant Pot alongside 1 to 2 cups of water. It is important the water level is not too high and touching the items being steamed, but there is enough water to last throughout the steaming process as steam will be escaping during the cook cycle. The Instant Pot glass lid, which must be purchased separately, is used to cover the Instant Pot and hold in the steam. To use Regular Steam, you will not be using the Steam function but rather the Sauté/Brown function of the Instant Pot. By setting the Sauté/Brown to High, the Instant Pot will heat the water until it boils and turns into steam, then continue to boil the rest of the water. Once the items are steamed to the desired doneness, you can easily extract them by removing the glass lid and the steamer insert.

In the Regular Steam function, there is a slight temperature difference between the base of the Instant Pot versus the top with the glass lid. You can use this to your advantage by stacking different sized items, or foods requiring slightly different steam times, into the Instant Pot from those needing the longest time (or largest cuts) at the bottom to those needing the shortest time (or smallest cuts) at the top.

How to Use the Pressure Steam Function

The Pressure Steam function on the Instant Pot works a little differently than the Regular Steam. In this scenario, a steamer insert—again either the metal trivet included with the Instant Pot or a standing basket-type insert purchased separately—is placed into the Instant Pot alongside a minimum 1 cup of water. You will need less liquid in the Pressure Steam scenario because the original Instant Pot lid creates an airtight seal, so there is no evaporation during the steaming process. Once the lid is locked and the pressure release valve set to Sealing, the Instant Pot again heats up the inner chamber to boil the water and convert that into steam. However, because the Instant Pot is *also* building pressure in this scenario, the water boils at a higher temperature—230°F (110°C) in the Low setting and 242°F (116°C) in the High setting—resulting in hotter steam than when cooking using the Regular Steam function. This means items will be cooked significantly faster during Pressure Steam. The main difference between the Steam function versus the Pressure Cook function is that the Instant Pot begins to heat at full power immediately, as it assumes there is only water in the inside chamber, versus in Pressure Cook the appliance will alternate through different power levels to avoid burning any food touching the bottom of the inner chamber. Once the Pressure Steam cycle is complete, it's also important to immediately Quick Release the pressure release valve to halt the cooking process and retain the structural integrity of the foods being steamed. Please be careful, as the liquid within the inner chamber may sputter during the release.

The Pressure Steam function is much more intense than Regular Steam, which is why Instant Pot's makers generally recommend using it for steaming frozen items or large foods. While you can certainly steam non-frozen foods and items you would handle with Regular Steam using Pressure Steam, it may take a few tries to best calculate the proper steam time. For a timetable comparing the steam times for Regular Steam versus Pressure Steam, please refer to our table on page 59 as a starting point. It's also important to note that Pressure Steam involves pressure building inside the Instant Pot and taking up space within the inner chamber. For certain foods that are meant to rise during the steaming process, like steamed cakes, the pressure will inhibit the rising of said item and the Quick Release at the end of the cycle will again deflate any part that has risen.

However, the Pressure Steam function is very useful as an alternative to microwaving foods to reheat them. Once the trivet has been set and water has been added, heat-proof containers such as Pyrex or Ball mason jars can be placed on top and steamed to reheat. This type of reheating method is much more even than using the microwave and sometimes faster than the oven or stovetop. A good starting point for most foods is 5 minutes of Pressure Steam time. It's also a good idea to wrap foods with foil to prevent condensation from the lid from dripping into the food, and moistening dry foods (such as a meatloaf) with some water before reheating to avoid further draining the water content during the reheat. Once complete, either a Quick Release or a Natural Pressure Release is suitable.

Important Tips for Steaming

These steaming tips are inclusive of both Regular Steam and Pressure Steam.

- Foods should be cut into similarly sized pieces to ensure even steaming.
- Foods should be placed with room on all sides to allow steam to reach all angles of the food and cook it evenly.
- Foods should be arranged in one layer when steaming to ensure consistent steam circulation. If you have multiple racks, each rack can hold one layer of food.
- Always open the lid *away* from your face. Remember that steam is hotter than water and there will be plenty of steam left in the inner chamber of the Instant Pot, regardless of when using Regular Steam or Pressure Steam.
- When cooking with Regular Steam, avoid removing the glass lid too frequently to check on your food, as it dramatically drops the temperature inside the Instant Pot.
- All foods will continue to cook slightly after the cooking process is stopped simply due to the hot temperature inside the food itself (known as "carryover cooking"). If you are attempting to judge the proper time to steam

an item, stop the steaming process when foods are at their brightest color and remove them from the heat source immediately to allow for minimum carryover.

Basic Steam Cooker Time Chart

Food Item	Regular Steam	Pressure Steam
Root vegetables (e.g., carrots, potatoes)	8–15 minutes	4–6 minutes
Leafy greens (e.g., spinach, kale)	3–5 minutes	Not advisable to pressure steam
Delicate vegetables (e.g., zucchini, leeks)	4–8 minutes	1–3 minutes
Fruit (e.g., cantaloupe, apple)	2–3 minutes	2–4 minutes
Eggs (hard boiled)	12 minutes	5 minutes
Eggs (soft boiled)	6 minutes	3 minutes
Chicken, breast	10–15 minutes	6–8 minutes
Fish, whole	8–12 minutes	4–5 minutes
Fish, fillet	4–8 minutes	1–3 minutes
Hardy vegetables (e.g., broccoli, cauliflower)	6–10 minutes	2–4 minutes
Shellfish	8–10 minutes	2–3 minutes
Chicken, thighs	20–30 minutes	8–10 minutes
Chicken, whole, 3–4 lbs	45–60 minutes	30 minutes

Common Questions and Troubleshooting

My steamed vegetables are too mushy!

Your vegetables have likely steamed too long. If using Regular Steam, remove 3 to 4 minutes from your cook cycle. If using Pressure Steam, remove 1 to 2 minutes from your cook cycle for next time.

Can I reheat frozen cooked items using the Pressure Steam function?

Absolutely! Place the food onto the trivet, or a basket, into the Instant Pot with at least 1 cup of water. Lock the lid and set to Sealing, then enter the time you would like the program to run.

Can I steam frozen items using the Regular Steam function?

Absolutely! You would follow the same process as above, but use the slow cooker lid instead of the locking pressure cooker lid. You'll need to significantly increase the amount of time your food is being steamed—a good amount to start is to double the time.

Should I boil the water before adding the steamer insert when cooking with Regular Steam?

You can boil the water to help speed up the process, but it is not necessary.

How do I know how much water to add when cooking with the Regular Steam function?

A good minimum amount of water is 1½ cups to start, but the final amount of water depends on how long you will be steaming. Because there is evaporation in the Regular Steam function, the longer foods are being steamed, the more water should be added to the chamber.

My steamed cheesecakes are flat. Why?

The Pressure Steam function still builds pressure inside the Instant Pot's chamber, which pushes down any steamed items attempting to inflate. If you are making steamed items that are meant to puff during the cooking process, switch to the Regular Steam function.

SAUTÉ/BROWN

The Sauté/Brown function on the Instant Pot is the one of the more straightforward of its functions and mimics the standard sautéing process on a stovetop pretty well. This chapter will break down the different presets available under Sauté/Brown, a few differences between sautéing in the Instant Pot versus traditional gas or electric stovetop, some sneaky ways the Sauté/Brown function can be used to utilize Instant Pot to its fullest, as well as common questions and troubleshooting.

How Sautéing Works

Sautéing is the cooking technique of using a small amount of oil to quickly cook food over a direct heat source like a stovetop or induction burner, typically set at a relatively high temperature. The idea of sautéing is to cook foods quickly in order to retain the moisture, texture, and color of the ingredients. The word *sauté* originates from the French verb "sauter," or "to jump," and refers to the that fact foods being sautéed are usually flipped or tossed in the pan, a motion most of us have seen set in slow-motion against flames in dramatic cooking videos.

The goal of sautéing is to transfer heat as quickly and evenly as possible to the food in order to trigger the Maillard reaction, where the protein and sugar molecules rearrange and bond in a way that changes the flavor and texture of the end product. The crisp sear on a steak, or browning of caramelized onions, or the aromas of roasted coffee are examples of Maillard at work. One of the easiest ways to achieve the Maillard reaction is to cook at high temperatures—past 280°F (137°C)—in a dry environment *or* at lower temperatures with more water.

In the case of sautéing, reducing the moisture available in the cooking environment is important, otherwise the food would be trapped under the boiling temperature of water at 212°F (100°C). Hence, the reason sautéing generally happens in a shallow pan. The two favorites for sautéing are a skillet (also known as a frying pan) or a sauté pan. The shallowness of both pans allow for quick moisture evaporation, ensuring foods being sautéed do not become damp and soggy but instead have a defined sear on the edges. Both pans are flat-bottomed, with the main difference being the angle of the sides of the pan: skillets have straight sides that fan outwards from the base, whereas sauté pans have straight sides that stand vertically from the base. Skillets allow for a more dexterous sautéing motion, given its angled edges, but sauté pans can hold more liquid and offer the use of a lid for slower evaporation. Because skillets lose a small amount of space from the base diameter due to its sloped sides, sauté pans of the same size offer a larger base—but are also much heavier. Ultimately, the two work equally well for the method of sautéing.

How Sauté/Brown on Instant Pot Differs from Traditional Methods

The Instant Pot maintains most functionalities of sautéing in most settings: it offers high temperatures and even distribution of heat. However, there are some key differences that's pertinent for Instant Pot users to know when they are facing an opportune scenario in which to use the Sauté/Brown function. The first is the high walls. As described above, sautéing typically happens in shallow pans to allow for evaporation. When using the Instant Pot, much more moisture builds up inside the chamber during the sautéing process. This does not mean ingredients cannot reach the temperature necessary for the Maillard process, but the results of certain sauté functions, especially searing and browning, will be less vivid when conducted in an Instant Pot. It is still perfectly good for tasks such as sweating onions and garlic, making a pan sauce, or sautéing ground beef. On the positive side, this means there is also much less oil splatter than in typical sautéing or pan frying, making the Instant Pot a great vessel for shallow-fried favorites such as stuffed zucchini blossoms. Please note pan-frying uses only a small amount of oil and is generally safe for the Instant Pot whereas deep-frying is not advisable.

> Pan-frying is generally safe
> for the Instant Pot; deep-frying
> is not advisable.

Another thing to take note of is the fact the bottom of the Instant Pot is not completely flat—the center is slightly higher than the sides to allow for space between the base of the chamber and the heating mechanism. This means the oil being used to sauté will tend to pool in the lower valleys of the chamber, thus requiring Instant Pot users to either add a touch more oil to form an even layer or move around the ingredients being sautéed more to ensure even cooking.

The final major difference is the consistency of the heat source. The Instant Pot offers three temperature settings on its Sauté/Brown function:

- Less: 221°F (105°C)
- Normal: 320°F (160°C)
- More: 338°F (170°C)

Once the desired setting has been selected, the Instant Pot will preheat the base to the corresponding tempera-ture and maintain that temperature for the duration of the cook time. The HOT warning will appear on the Instant Pot once the preheat is finished, and the setting cook time is 30 minutes for Sauté/Brown, after which it resets. Because the heating mechanism keeps the same temperature, there is less variable temperature during the entire sauté process. This is good for even cooking, especially because there are no hot spots in any part of the pan or heat source, but also means there is no easy or quick recalibration of temperature inside the chamber. If too many ingredients are added to the Instant Pot too quickly (known as "overcrowding"), the entire tempera-ture of the inner chamber will drop and it will take some time to bring the temperature back to its original point, even if you toggle between settings, such as moving from Less to More. If something inside the Instant Pot is too hot, it also takes more time to cool down despite switching from setting to setting. In this sense, sautéing in the Instant Pot requires a little more exacting of volume and quantity of food being cooked, as it is less forgiving—or as easily transferable—than cooking on a traditional stovetop.

Clever Ways to Use Sauté/Brown on Instant Pot

There are many ways to utilize the Sauté/Brown function on the Instant Pot, especially to reduce the amount of pots and pans used to prepare a meal. Some particularly efficient tasks are:

- Reducing leftover liquid from a completed pressure cook to create a jus for serving
- Making a pan sauce using leftover liquid after a completed pressure cook by adding a thickener (such as cornstarch or roux)
- Using leftover liquid from a completed pressure cook to steam ingredients
- Sautéing aromatics such as spices or sweating onions and garlic prior to starting a pressure cook or slow cook
- Searing or browning meats prior to starting a pressure cook or slow cook
- Reheating foods more quickly than the Warming function, either directly in the chamber or by heating water under the Sauté setting and sealed foods (i.e., vacuum-packed or canned) into the chamber

Common Questions and Troubleshooting

My sauté function won't start!
The Sauté function will not start on the Instant Pot if your lid is on. Remove the lid and press Sauté/Brown again.

When do I know the Instant Pot has preheated to the given sauté temperature?
The Instant Pot will display the word HOT when fully preheated.

How long is a Sauté mode?
The Sauté mode is 30 minutes, after which it resets. This means you will need to press Sauté/Brown again and select your temperature setting; however, if you do this quickly after the mode resets, there should be no additional preheat time.

When should I add oil to the Instant Pot?
You can add oil to the Instant Pot as it is preheating and let it come to the correct temperature alongside the inner chamber.

What temperature should I sauté vegetables?
Most vegetables sauté well on the Normal temperature setting, with time adjustments made for size and structure of the vegetable, but it depends on your desired end effect on the vegetables. Caramelized onions, for instance, should cook slowly on the Less setting over a long period of time whereas browned potatoes should be sautéed on the More setting.

What temperature should I sear meats?
Meats should be seared on the More setting, after the oil has been given ample time to heat up and mirror the desired temperature.

My Instant Pot won't start pressure cooking after I use the Sauté/Brown function!
There is a safety precaution built into the Instant Pot that requires the heating mechanism to cool to a certain temperature before a new, different cook mode can be selected after the Sauté/Brown process has completed. Simply wait a few minutes if your Instant Pot won't readily switch to a new cook mode.

What should I do with my leftover oil from sautéing?
In most instances, after the Instant Pot and oil has cooled completely, you can strain leftover oil through a fine-mesh strainer or cheesecloth and save it for another use. This oil can be stored at room temperature until the next use, within three months or so. However, this is not recommended for leftover oil from sautéing raw meats, especially poultry or fish.

KEEP WARM

The Keep Warm function on the Instant Pot has one set temperature but allows flexibility in time. It's an extremely useful way to keep food warm after being cooked (in an Instant Pot or otherwise) or rewarm it from a cold state. This chapter will break down what the Keep Warm function does both by itself and as part of other Instant Pot functions, as well as common questions and troubleshooting.

Using the Manual Keep Warm Setting on Instant Pot

The Keep Warm setting on the Instant Pot operates between 145°F to 172°F (62°C to 77°C), which is squarely outside of the "Temperature Danger Zone" where bacteria multiplies exponentially (40°F to 140°F, or 4°C to 60°C). When the Keep Warm setting is accessed on the Instant Pot manually as its own specific function, you can customize the amount of time the Instant Pot is keeping food warm inside the chamber—anything from 1 minute to 99 hours and 50 minutes. You can keep warm foods warm, or reheat cold foods, either directly in the chamber or in heat-safe containers such as Pyrex containers or Ball mason jars set onto a trivet inside the Instant Pot with enough water to match the level of the food. The Keep Warm setting can be used with the lid both on or off the Instant Pot. However, it is important to factor in evaporation if the lid is off and food is being warmed for long periods of time.

Using the Default Keep Warm Setting after Other Cook Programs

The Keep Warm setting will automatically turn on after other cook programs have completed in the Instant Pot. The automatic time for this setting is 10 hours and cannot be adjusted unless you switch to the manual Keep Warm setting. This is useful for those who want to start the cook process in the morning and come home to a warm meal for lunch or dinner. If you want to turn *off* the Keep Warm setting after a cook program, you will need to deselect the Keep Warm setting when entering the time for your primary cook program (typically, the light for Keep Warm is lit to indicate the program will kick into Keep Warm after it's complete). This makes sense if you are cooking delicate items, such as eggs, and do not want the Instant Pot to keep cooking the food if you forget to remove them from the chamber immediately.

Common Questions and Troubleshooting

Is Keep Warm the fastest way to reheat my cold food?
No, using the Keep Warm function is arguably the slowest

way to reheat cold food due to its low temperature. Using the Pressure Steam is an efficient and much faster way to reheat cold food. However, Keep Warm is very useful for reheating cold food in a slow, even way, which is useful for delicate items such as green sauces and to keep food warm for a very long period of time.

When should I turn off the default Keep Warm function after a cook cycle is complete?

It's a good idea to turn off the default Keep Warm function if you are cooking delicate foods that are easily overcooked such as eggs, lean proteins and fish, baked pastries, or tender vegetables.

How do I lengthen the amount of time Keep Warm is on past 10 hours?

In order to use Keep Warm past the default 10 hours, you must switch to the manual Keep Warm function after the cook cycle is complete. Unfortunately, this means you must be in front of the Instant Pot when the initial cook cycle finishes and the default Keep Warm kicks in so you can cancel that setting and switch to the manual Keep Warm function.

Does Keep Warm always keep my food at the same temperature?

You are able to adjust the temperature controls for the Keep Warm setting on later versions of the Instant Pot, from Less to More, depending at which temperature you would like to keep your food.

CAKE MAKER AND STERILIZE

This chapter covers two advanced settings and functions available in certain models of the Instant Pot: the Cake Maker and Sterilize settings.

Cake Maker

Cake Maker is a preset setting available on almost all newer versions of the Instant Pot. It uses the same Pressure Cook function but has helpful preset times and pressure settings to bake different types of cakes. **Please note there is an error in certain Instant Pot manuals that denote a No Pressure option for the Cake Maker setting. This is incorrect, and Instant Pot has since redacted that information. However, in the Ultra models you *can* use the Steam function under no pressure.** This section will explain the different pressures and temperatures available for the Cake Maker setting, how the Instant Pot's cake "baking" differs from traditional baking in an oven, as well as common questions and troubleshooting.

How Traditional Baking Works

Baking is a dry-heat cooking method that transfers high heat—typically 300°F or above—indirectly from the heat source to the food by containing the food in an enclosed vessel, typically an oven. The heat cooks the food from the outside in, resulting in an exterior that is dryer, firmer, and browner than the inside. The term *baking* differentiates from roasting, as it refers to food items that start with limited structure (e.g., cake batter) and, through the process of baking, develops a more stable construction. During this process, other important changes also take place within the food item that contribute to the final product: solid fats melt, sugar dissolves, gluten and dairy proteins coagulate, microorganisms (such as yeast) die off, and the Maillard reaction takes place. As discussed on page 64, one of the easiest ways to achieve the Maillard reaction is to cook at high temperatures—past 280°F (137°C)—which is exactly why the outside of foods brown and develop a deeper flavor over the course of the baking process.

The main differentiator of the baking process is the distribution of dry heat over and through the food being cooked. However, some baked items do use a small amount of moisture in the process by placing the baked item in a vessel within a larger vessel filled with water (the bain-marie method). This method is used for more delicate baked items, such as soufflés or custards, as the water acts as an additional temper for the indirect, but still intense, heat inside the oven. The end result is a fluffier, moister baked item that has set more softly than one baked without the water bath.

How the Instant Pot Cake Maker Works

The Cake Maker setting on the Instant Pot is not "baking" by circulating dry, hot air around the food to cook it. Instead, it is utilizing the same function as Pressure Cook by heating water past its boiling temperature and using the resulting steam to cook the food. Perhaps a better title for the setting would be Cake Steamer. Because of this, cakes cooked in the Instant Pot will not take on many of the typical characteristics of baked goods. Overall, it is advisable to replicate desserts that take well to moist cooking methods or traditionally use the bain-marie in the Instant Pot—steamed cakes, pudding cakes, custards—instead of baked items that prize a crusty, flaky, or crumbly texture, such as baguettes, cobblers, and pies.

When comparing Instant Pot finished cakes to traditional baked cakes, you'll find significantly less browning to the exterior of the cake. Although the Maillard reaction can happen at lower temperatures with more water, due to the short amount of time and small amount of water being used in most Instant Pot cake recipes, the Maillard often does not occur. The other changes, like fats melting or sugar dissolving, still take place, as there is enough of a temperature increase. Finished cakes are also usually moister than their baked counterparts, due to the fact Instant Pot "baking" requires the addition of water (to create steam) and there is no evaporation throughout the entire cooking process. This could either be a positive or a negative: perhaps a good result for a Bundt cake but not ideal for a crumble. However, it is useful to note that because this additional moisture is being incorporated into the final cake, recipes can use less fats—such as butter or egg yolk—to achieve the same texture.

Using the Cake Maker Setting

The Cake Maker setting draws upon the regular Pressure Cook function and thus can be used at two different pressures: High or Low. The vast majority of cake recipes for the Instant Pot calls for the High Pressure setting, allowing users to shave time off a traditional baked cake recipe while still resulting in a moist cake. "Baking" in the Instant Pot will generally need only half the cook time listed in a traditional oven-baked recipe. The Low Pressure setting does not save any cooking time but can be useful for desserts meant to be very soft, airy, and moist—soufflés, sponge cakes, custards—where the High Pressure may deflate the rising process or break the delicate air pockets formed within the cake.

Most Instant Pot cake recipes will use the *pot in pot* method, where cakes are baked inside of another heat-safe, enclosed vessel while perched on the trivet. This way, the second vessel is not submerged in the boiling water and not directly making contact with the heat source at the bottom of the Instant Pot. It is important to use vessels that can withstand high temperatures, such as oven-safe ramekins and baking dishes, to ensure nothing breaks while being cooked inside the Instant Pot. For certain baking dishes that do not come with a built-in cover, the cake batter still must be covered with foil to prevent condensation from the Instant Pot's lid from dripping down on the top of the batter and impacting the final consistency of the cake, or many times causing it to not rise at all. It's particularly useful to fashion an aluminum "sling," akin to a holding basket, to encase uncovered vessels for easier removal once cooking is complete. All Instant Pot cake recipes will require at least 1 cup of water at the bottom of the inner chamber to start the cook process.

Once the pressure has been selected, you are also able to adjust the temperature to Less, Normal, or More options and select a time range up to 4 hours. The below are general suggestions for the types of cakes best suited for each option, assuming High Pressure has been selected. In Low Pressure scenarios, work from Less to More depending on just how delicate the food is. Make sure your pressure valve is set to Sealing.

- **Less:** Best for lightly cooked desserts, such as pudding cakes, desserts containing delicate ingredients that do not stand up to higher temperatures (e.g., coconut oil), and airier desserts like angel food cake. You will likely need to add some cooking time when using this mode.
- **Normal:** Best for moist but still bouncy desserts of similar consistency as a typical boxed cake or Bundt cake.
- **More:** Best for dense, wetter desserts such as cheesecake, chocolate lava cake, banana bread, and brownies. You may need to remove some cooking time when using this mode.

Once the cook cycle is complete, a good general rule is to use Natural Pressure Release for risen desserts (like cakes) to avoid deflating the food in this last step and Quick

Release for items such as brownies or puddings where the height of the final item is less important. However, for cakes of sturdier construction or desserts easy to over-cook, Quick Release could be a better option. Since most cakes will not have achieved the standard browning on its exterior, many Instant Pot bakers will either frost or glaze their finished cakes to mask this effect, or flash-brown the cake in the oven by baking it at a high temperature (450°F or 230°C).

Cake Maker: Common Questions and Troubleshooting

What's the best kinds of desserts to make in my Instant Pot?

Moist desserts that are traditionally made with the bain-marie method, or are usually steamed, work particularly well in the Instant Pot. Other desserts that are prized for a richer, wetter texture like pudding cakes also make a lot of sense.

What's the difference between the Instant Pot Cake Maker setting and the regular Pressure Cook function?

The Cake Maker setting uses the Pressure Cook function but offers slightly more control over the final cooking temperature in the inner chamber.

Will my desserts cook faster in the Instant Pot than in the oven?

Some desserts will cook faster in the Instant Pot when cooked on High Pressure, but this is not always the case. A good rule of thumb when cooking on High Pressure is to halve the time allocated to a traditional oven-bake of that item, then assess its doneness. In Low Pressure scenarios, the cook times in an Instant Pot versus in an oven will be roughly the same.

Can I cook cakes in the Instant Pot without any water?

No. The Instant Pot's Cake Maker setting uses the Pressure Cook function, which requires some type of water in the inner chamber in order to create hot steam to cook the food. The Instant Pot will not start without water in this situation, and there is no way to exactly mimic the dry heat of a traditional oven using the Instant Pot's Cake Maker setting.

Can I place the container with the batter directly into the inner chamber without the trivet when cooking in the Instant Pot?

No. This direct contact between the inside vessel and the stainless steel of the inside chamber could be very dangerous when combined with high heat from the heat source at the bottom of the Instant Pot.

Can I pour cake batter directly into the Instant Pot's inner chamber?

Yes, *but* this will likely not result in the desired outcome for the cake, because the Instant Pot will be boiling the cake batter to create sufficient steam to cook the rest of the ingredients. It's also likely there is not even liquid inside the cake batter to boil appropriately, and the entire cake batter may burn.

My Instant Pot cakes didn't rise! Why?

For cakes where height is important, it's best to use Natural Pressure Release to ensure the forced venting of a Quick Release does not deflate the cake. Cake batter should also be protected from the condensation of the Instant Pot lid using a cover or aluminum foil. Delicate desserts with limited leavening agents—such as soufflés, which only use egg whites—should be cooked on the lowest, gentlest setting possible: Low Pressure on Less temperature.

My Instant Pot cakes are soggy! Why?

Cooking desserts in the Instant Pot tends to add some moisture to the final product, as they are in a wet cooking environment. If cakes are soggy or too dense, you may need to reduce the amount of wet ingredients or the fat content of your recipe. Alternatively, if only the top of your cake is soggy, it is because the top of the batter was not shielded from the condensation of the Instant Pot's lid.

Sterilize

The Sterilize setting is new for Instant Pot models Ultra and Plus and has quickly become a favorite for new parents and pickling/fermentation enthusiasts. This section will explain the use case and process for sterilization, pasteurization, and boiling water canning, how to do each effectively in the Instant Pot, and will end with common questions and troubleshooting.

What Is Sterilization and Pasteurization?

Sterilization is the process of destroying any living or dormant microorganisms existing in a particular space or food by causing irreversible denaturation of its enzymes and structural proteins. This can be done by various heating methods—moist heat, dry heat, direct or indirect heat—depending on which type of microorganisms you are targeting. Temperatures of 175°F (80°C) is enough to destroy active bacteria, yeast, and fungi that may exist in your food; boiling water (212°F or 100°C) kills most other forms of pathogenic bacteria; while temperatures above 240°F (116°C) is needed to destroy dormant organisms. Traditional methods of sterilization include boiling, steaming, and baking items at the temperature required for sterilization. The steaming method, which is what Instant Pot's Sterilize function utilizes, is the most common and generally seen as the most consistent and dependable. Steam sterilization provides precise temperature controls, heats very quickly, and is inexpensive to replicate widely.

When sterilizing food itself, factors such as type of food, acidity level, sealing method, and shelf life must be taken into consideration to minimize damage to the final food product while keeping it safe for consumption. We will discuss this in more detail in the Boiling Water Canning section or as well as in the section on Pressure Canning, starting on page 100.

Food containers and other items that are often sterilized are those meant to house food where bacterial content must be carefully controlled. For example, baby bottles or sippy cups for newborns must be void of all bacteria as babies, especially those too young to be vaccinated, are very susceptible to infections. Storage jars for pickling or fermenting enthusiasts, or equipment for homebrewers, should be sterilized to ensure only the proper bacteria is then incorporated into the final food product. While not necessary, it's also a good idea to sterilize most food storage containers regularly.

Pasteurization is similar to the sterilization in the fact its goal is to also make food safer for consumption by utilizing heat to kill unfavorable bacteria such as *E. coli*. However, pasteurization uses much lower temperatures than sterilization and thereby still leaves some living organisms in the food. This means pasteurized food still needs to be kept refrigerated and has a shorter shelf life than sterilized food (but a longer shelf life than its unpasteurized counterparts). The most commonly pasteurized food product is milk, which you may also be using the Instant Pot for, as well as juices or meats, fish, and eggs meant to be eaten on the raw or rare side. Pasteurization is especially important for those whose immune systems may be compromised: pregnant women, young children, the elderly, or those with immune deficiency disorders. It also helps break down some of the proteins in the food being heated, which aids in digestion. Note that pasteurization refers to an act done onto a food product, not an item or container, whereas sterilization can refer to either.

What Is Boiling Water Canning?

Boiling water canning (BWC) is one method of food preservation that uses boiling water to create an airtight seal inside a glass jar. This method is meant for high-acid foods such as fruit jams and jellies, fermented foods with lactic acid and pickled items, because the high acid content minimizes the risk for botulism, a poisoning caused by the toxin from *Clostridium botulinum*. Acidity is measured on the pH scale, where acidity increases as the pH *decreases*, and vice versa. A pH below 4.6 is ideal for the BWC method. Some fruits, such as tomatoes and figs, have low acidity (sometimes more than 4.6), are best canned with an additional acidic ingredient to ensure safety. Low acid foods include most vegetables and certainly all meats, dairy, and fish. These must be processed using Pressure Canning to ensure safety, which we will cover on page 100.

The traditional process of BWC is straightforward. First, food is placed in clean (preferably sterilized) mason or canning jars with metal lids and a metal screw band. Home canners can choose between raw-packing or hot-packing foods, both of which are suitable for BWC—*raw-packed* means fresh (or raw) food is placed into the jar and boiling liquid is poured on top whereas *hot-packed* means food is heated in boiling water, then packed into the jars. All packed food should be left with some headspace, ¼ inch to ½ inch, to allow for a proper seal and accompanying metal bands adjusted snugly—"fingertip tight" is the rule of thumb—to avoid leaking. Jars are then placed into a canner, or simply a large pot with a trivet or rack, and covered with water to at least 1 inch above the top of the jars. The water is then heated to boiling and kept at boiling for the amount of time specified per canning recipe.

Once complete, jars are carefully removed with tongs and set on a heat-safe surface to rest for 24 hours. A good sign of a proper seal is a pinging sound and a concave dip in the metal lids. After 24 hours, you can check for proper seals by unscrewing the metal band and attempting to lift the jars off the counter using your fingertips on the lid. If the lid stays intact without issue, a seal has formed and the canned food can be safely kept at room temperature. If not, you can re-can the food or store in the refrigerator to be consumed quickly.

How to Use the Sterilize Setting on the Instant Pot

The Sterilize setting on the Instant Pot uses its Steam function to effectively raise the temperature inside the chamber to a level where harmful bacteria, active or dormant, will be killed. This presumes you will be sterilizing food inside of a sealed container, such as mason jars or cans, and will either be using the trivet included with the Instant Pot or a steamer insert of some variety. The Sterilize setting allows adjustment of the sterilization temperature from Less to More. Less is meant for pasteurization and heats to 161°F. Normal is meant to mimic BWC and heats to the temperature of boiling water (212°F or 100°C). And More is meant for sterilizing objects, heating steam to the 250°F range.

To use the Sterilize setting, add 2 cups of water to the inside chamber of the Instant Pot. Place the trivet or steamer basket into the Instant Pot and add in all the food or items that need to be pasteurized, canned, or sterilized. All food items should be separated into sealed containers and standing upright to prevent spillage. Nothing except the trivet or steamer basket should be touching the base of the inside chamber or the water. Select Sterilize and choose the proper temperature for what activity you're doing, then check the release valve is set to Sealing so the temperature can adequately build in the chamber. The timing of each process varies—typically 2 minutes for pasteurizing milk or sterilizing objects, and 10 minutes for canned items. Let the Instant Pot run through the cycle, then allow for a Natural Pressure Release. Carefully remove all items from the Instant Pot with tongs or heatproof mitts.

For sterilized items, dry and store in a clean area. For pasteurized food, cool the food to below the Temperature Danger Zone (40°F to 140°F) by submerging in an ice bath, then transferring to the refrigerator or freezer. It's important to cool the food as quickly as possible to minimize the amount of time it spends in the Danger Zone. For canned items, let cool at room temperature for 24 hours before testing the seal of each lid to ensure it has properly closed in. If you are using mason jars, you should be able to remove the metal rings and easily pick up the jar without the lid coming loose. Canned items can then be stored at room temperature for 3 to 5 years, depending on the condition of its storage area. If the seal is not complete, you can either reprocess the faulty jars in a jar with the same process or refrigerate and assume a shelf life similar to pasteurization.

Sterilize: Common Questions and Troubleshooting

Do higher altitudes affect sterilization and pasteurization?

Yes, higher altitudes impact sterilization and pasteurization because it changes the temperature in which water boils. Some models of the Instant Pot come with an altitude calibration, but for those that do not, it's important to refer to an altitude adjustment metric to change the processing time needed for sterilizing and pasteurizing.

What's the best environment to stored canned foods?
In a cool, dark, and dry place.

Can I store canned foods for longer than a year?
Some foods can be stored this long. There is no definitive answer on how long things can be stored, though typically canned foods are consumed within five years. You can judge for yourself after opening the canned item to determine if it is suitable for consumption.

How can I test the pH of my foods?
You can buy pH strips or a digital pH meter.

Is canning in the Instant Pot the same as Boiling Water Canning?
Not exactly. BWC uses the heat from boiling water to tightly seal the glass jars, whereas the Instant Pot uses the heat from the steam of boiling water to tightly seal the glass jars—also called steam canning. The two methods call for the same processing times and have the same results, but steam canning requires much less water.

What's the difference between milk pasteurized in the Instant Pot versus Ultra High Temperature pasteurized (UHT) milk?
The Instant Pot pasteurizes milk at a much lower temperature (161°F) than UHT pasteurized milk (275°F or more). This results in the retention of more nutrients and, some say, flavor of the milk.

My metal lids are not concave, but they are sealed. Is that okay?

As long as you can lift the jars by the metal lid without the lid coming loose, then yes.

The food I'm trying to can is right at the pH cutoff. Is that okay?

Yes, but if you are concerned, you can lower the pH by adding an acidifying agent like vinegar.

Can I pasteurize my milk at a lower temperature?

Yes, you can pasteurize milk at a lower temperature of 145°F. Typically when this is done, milk is held at this temperature for at least 30 minutes. The Instant Pot does not have this setting preset in Sterilize, but you can do so yourself using the Sauté function and measuring the temperature carefully with a digital thermometer.

How should I store sterilized objects?

In a cool and dry place with ventilation.

My canned jars didn't seal! Why?

There are a variety of reasons: check to make sure you have not overfilled your jars, that the metal screw is not too tight or too loose, that there is no rust on either the metal screw or lid, that the Instant Pot had enough water and processed the full Sterilize cycle.

SOUS VIDE AND PRESSURE CANNING

This chapter covers two advanced functions available in certain models of the Instant Pot: Sous Vide and Pressure Canning functions.

Sous Vide

A built-in Sous Vide function is available on the Instant Pot Smart and Max models, which calibrates the temperature of the inner chamber using the base heating mechanism. For those who do not have an Instant Pot Smart or Max, there is also an accessory called the Instant Pot SV800 Sous Vide Immersion Circulator that can be combined with the inner chamber of any Instant Pot to turn that into a sous vide machine. This chapter will explain how sous vide cooking works, the pros and cons of sous vide cooking, important considerations for cooking sous vide in the Instant Pot as well as common questions and troubleshooting. We will be focusing on the Instant Pot Smart and Max models built-in Sous Vide function in this chapter, but we discuss the separate Sous Vide Immersion Circulator accessory on page 111.

How Sous Vide Cooking Works

Sous vide, French for the term "under vacuum," is a method of cooking foods in water held at a precise temperature. The main tenets that differentiate sous vide from cooking food in water (e.g., boiling, poaching) are that foods are containerized in some way—typically vacuum-sealed in plastic—and temperature of the water is much lower than traditional methods. Instead of cooking the foods from the outside-in with high temperatures of water, the water is set at the final desired doneness temperature, which requires cooking the food for a much longer period of time. While the French terms refers to the vacuum-sealed nature of most of the foods being cooked sous vide, and the fact the forefathers of sous vide typically did both vacuum-sealing and sous vide cooking, vacuum-sealing is *not* required to cook foods sous vide, and in some instances, such as eggs, no sealing is required at all. Many will cook sous vide using resealable glass jars or even Ziploc bags. However, it is *recommended* food being cooked is vacuum-sealed because the removal of air from the bag ensures the most efficient thermal transfer from water heat to food, there is no loss of moisture as the juices and flavorings are pushed back into the food being cooked, and the lack of air minimizes bacterial growth and oxidation.

The best example of sous vide cooking is with meats generally cooked rare or medium rare (e.g., steak). By employing the sous vide method, these meats can be cooked to the desired doneness (i.e., 130°F for medium rare) without risk of overcooking or carryover cooking. When sliced, the meat will be visibly the same color along all sides whereas a traditionally cooked cut of meat will be only medium rare at the very center. These lower temperatures also ensure the cell walls in the food do not burst, which helps vegetables retain crispness even after being cooked and meats retain their moisture while still breaking down the collagen in connective tissues and turning it into edible gelatin. Sous vide is especially useful for oddly shaped food items, or cooking in large batches of slightly irregular items—the even temperature ensures foods both large, small, and misshapen will cook to the same degree of doneness. However, it is important to note that in many instances sous vide cooking does not result in the Maillard reaction, which usually takes place at higher temperatures (above 280°F, 137°C), meaning food cooked sous vide do not develop the classic roasted, toasty notes and brown color. If the temperature of the cooking process is low enough, fats may also not render and melt, as that happens in the 130°F to 140°F range. Many mitigate these two issues by selecting leaner cuts of meat, pre-searing meats to render some fat, or finishing sous vide items on an extremely hot grill or cast-iron pan after it is finished cooking (also known as "reverse searing").

The time required for sous vide cooking is also much longer than regular cooking methods—often 4× or more. A soft-boiled egg, for instance, takes only 8 minutes in boiling water, but 1 hour when cooked sous vide. This does mean planning in advance is required, and a higher amount of electricity is consumed during the cooking process. Final times and temperatures vary from food item to food item, and the amount of time needed to cook certain items does increase when the amount of food being cooked increases, or the thickness of meats increases. However, one of the benefits of sous vide cooking is that it is significantly more forgiving than regular cook methods—leaving items cooking sous vide for minutes, even hours, may sometimes have unnoticeable adverse impact on the final product. While it is technically not possible to "overcook" food using the sous vide method, past a certain point the food will break down so far it results in an undesirably mealy or mushy texture. For foods cooked sous vide, especially meat, it is still required to allow the meat to rest after removing it from its container—same as traditional cooking methods.

Sous vide and *immersion circulator* are often found in the same sentence. Sous vide is the cooking method, while immersion circulators are the tool used to create an environment conducive for sous vide cooking. Specifically, they are instruments that will heat and circulate water while keeping the temperature within a few degrees of the desired setting.

How to Use the Instant Pot's Sous Vide Function

The Instant Pot's Sous Vide function strives to do the same thing as most immersion circulators by keeping the temperature of water in the inner chamber consistent throughout the duration of the cooking process. However, the Instant Pot Sous Vide function is *not* an immersion circulator, meaning it does not move water consistently throughout the cooking process but instead still heats the water from the base heating mechanism and adjusts that temperature up or down as needed.

Thus, the temperature detected by the Instant Pot is an approximation of the overall water temperature and may vary from the bottom to the top of the inner chamber. The makers of the Instant Pot have stated they have performed numerous experiments and, most of the time, temperature in the Instant Pot Smart can be maintained within 1°C of the set temperature and the Max 0.5°C *but* the set temperature should be calibrated first. Do this using °C, not °F.

To calibrate the Instant Pot, fill the inner chamber with enough water to fully submerge the foods you will be cooking sous vide—usually at least halfway full. For the Smart model, download the Instant Pot Smart Cooker mobile app (available at Apple App Store or Google Play) and head to Settings. There, you should pair your app to the Instant Pot, then set the temperature units (°F or °C), adjust for elevation, and set your desired temperature (e.g., 60°C). In the Max model, select Sous Vide and set the temperature dial to your desired temperature. Once the Smart Cooker app or the Max's digital interface indicates it has heated the Instant Pot to that temperature, measure the temperature in the Instant Pot by inserting a food thermometer in the water. In some cases, the two temperatures will be different—for example, if you receive a 63°C result with your physical water test, now you know that the "set" temperature from the Instant Pot runs 3°C higher than your actual desired temperature and can adjust accordingly (i.e., set the Smart Cooker app to 57°C next time). This is by no means a perfect method, which is why the makers of Instant Pot recommend only using the Sous Vide function for food items that are not too sensitive to slight temperature differences.

On page 111, under "Accessories," we will cover the Instant Pot Immersion Circulator, which acts much more similarly to a traditional regular immersion circulator on the market and offers greater consistency for sous vide cooking.

Sous Vide: Common Questions and Troubleshooting

Is it safe to cook food in plastic?

While we cannot scientifically say yes with 100 percent backing from all medical journals, the overwhelming majority of plastics research says yes. However, not all plastic is made equal, so it's important to make sure the plastic you are using to encase your foods being cooked sous vide is food-grade plastic.

Can I use Ziploc bags to cook sous vide?

Assuming you are comfortable cooking with plastic (see above) then yes, Ziploc bags are a perfectly good choice to use for cooking sous vide. However, make sure to use the food-grade, freezer-style bags, as they are the most temperature resistant. It is important to note that above 158°F (70°C), the seams of Ziploc bags may begin to weaken and open, which compromises the food you are cooking. If you will be cooking food sous vide above this temperature, opt for a heavier-duty sous vide specific bag *or* double-bag your Ziploc bags.

What kind of jars can I use to cook sous vide?

The same kind of jars you would use for canning—mason jars or Ball jars are both good candidates.

What types of food is best to cook using sous vide?
Any food you would like to cook with great precision (and have some time to spare to get it perfectly right!). Meats that are typically served medium and under are great candidates, as well as foods that overcook easily (fish, chicken). Vegetables that tend to lose their crunch when cooked (asparagus, broccoli) are also great, as are anything involving eggs—custards, ice cream bases, even flan.

How should I season food that I'm going to cook sous vide?
Season your food normally when cooking sous vide, as you would if cooking in traditional methods. It is important to note that because the food is sealed in tightly with the seasonings, it will likely infuse a little more than usual into the food, so if you're unsure, go with a pinch less versus more.

I don't have a vacuum sealer. How do I seal food I'm going to cook sous vide?
You can use the water displacement method. First, you place the food you want to cook into the Ziploc bag with the seal open. Next, you place that into the water (carefully) until the food is fully submerged—you'll see that water will displace the air around the food in the bag and create a "seal" of sorts. Continue submerging the bag into the water until you reach the seam, then tightly close up the Ziploc and let it cook!

Can I reheat my food using sous vide?
Absolutely! A good temperature to reheat food is in the 130°F to 140°F (55°C to 60°C) range.

Can I cook store-bought frozen items using sous vide?
Yes, you can take frozen items in the bag and cook directly in the sous vide. However, this means you do not have the opportunity to season the frozen food. Frozen foods also take more time to cook sous vide; a good rule of thumb is to double the cooking time.

How do I do a "reverse sear" on my meats I cooked sous vide?

Once your meat has finished cooking, remove from the plastic bag and pat dry with a paper towel. Next, heat up neutral oil with a high smoking point (e.g., canola oil not extra virgin olive oil) in a suitably sized fry pan (preferably cast-iron) until it is almost smoking, then add your meat and sear 1 to 2 minutes on each side, or until you develop the level of brownness desired. For thinner pieces of meat, be careful not to overcook during this step! After searing, let the meat rest before slicing, as you would a traditionally cooked piece of meat.

Should I add oil to my sous vide bag?
It depends on what you're making. It's usually a good idea to include at least 1 tablespoon of oil to help things in the sous vide bags move around and not congeal during the cooking process. Sous vide is a great way to confit items, such as duck legs, with significantly less oil than the traditional version (usually a quarter or so of the regular amount). However, some users have said adding oil alongside spices and herbs dilutes the final flavor of the main item being cooked, as some of those spices and herbs infuse the oil instead—so it's very much a personal preference.

How many items can I cook sous vide at once?

This also depends on how large the container you're using to sous vide is. It's important to not overcrowd the container—if using the Instant Pot, this causes higher variation of water temperature from the base to the top; if using an immersion circulator, this prevents the water from moving freely around the container and also causes temperature stabilization issues. A good rule of thumb is that all the items being cooked sous vide are not all squished against each other in the container.

My sous vide meat is under/overcooked! Why?

Depending on how thick or thin the cut of meat you have is, it may need less or more time in sous vide than the recipe calls for. It's best to use the recipe times as a jumping-off off point, then to calculate a final time based on total weight of your food item. When in doubt, it's always easier to go a little longer than shorter!

My sous vide meat has chewy fat on it! Why?

Fat begins to melt in the 130°F to 140°F range, so if your final temperature is lower than that (or just on the cusp), some fat may still remain on your meat after the sous vide cook is over. A good way to get around this issue is to either pre-sear or reverse sear your meat items and to choose leaner cuts of meat to sous vide.

My sous vide meat is mushy! Why?

While sous vide cooking cannot technically overcook your food, food that has been left too long will still begin to disintegrate as the cellular structure is compromised. This results in an unappetizing texture many refer to as mushy. If this is the case, reduce your cooking times.

My vegetables keep floating when I try to cook them sous vide.

Vegetables are more susceptible to floating when being cooked sous vide. There are many workarounds for this. The easiest three are: adding a heavy item to the bag (e.g., a spoon) to cause it to sink, using sous vide ping-pong balls to line the top of the water or using sous vide racks and tying each bag to the rack.

Pressure Canning

The Pressure Canning function is new for Instant Pot Max and still under debate over safety. This section will explain the difference between pressure canning versus boiling water canning (covered on page 84), how to pressure can in the Instant Pot (if you are comfortable with the risks), as well as common questions and troubleshooting.

What is Pressure Canning?

Pressure Canning is a food preservation method used to process food items that are low-acid (higher than 4.6 pH). Most vegetables and all meats, dairy, and seafood products fall into this category. It is imperative these food items are pressure canned, versus using BWC, because there is not enough natural acid to prevent the growth of *Clostridium botulinum*, more colloquially known as botulism, which is extremely dangerous and can cause lasting nerve damage. In order to kill off the *Clostridium botulinum*, the temperature needs to reach the 240°F to 250°F (115°C to 120°C) range, which is higher than the boiling point of water (212°F or 100°C)—thus, the need for additional pressure. The amount of time needed to kill off all bacteria during pressure canning ranges from 20 minutes to over 2 hours—variations depend on factors such as what is being pressure canned, size of jars, and how the jars were packed. Adjustments also must be made for those who live at higher altitudes, where water boils at a lower temperature and thus changes the amount of pressure needed to reach the desired pressure canning temperature.

Traditional pressure canning uses one of two types of pressure canners: one outfitted with a dial gauge or a weighted gauge. A weighted gauge pressure canner automatically senses the pressure inside the chamber and will shift to allow venting if the pressure begins to build past the set pressure and final temperature. The dial gauge version requires the user to monitor the pressure and manually change the heat source in order to keep the pressure at the right level. Occasionally, dial gauge pressure canners also need to be recalibrated.

On the exception of the pressure measuring device, both types of pressure canners work similarly. The first few steps mirror those for boiling water canning: filling food in clean (or sterilized) suitably sized canning jars—raw-packed or hot-packed—with proper headspace and a snug seal. Jars must sit on a rack or trivet in the pressure canner, not stand directly on the base, and water added to the chamber. It's important the jars have space between them so steam can surround all the jars. At this point, the two paths diverge. For pressure canning, a cover is placed onto the pressure canner and pressure escape valve set to the Venting position. Heat is applied, either from a separate source such as a stovetop or internally from the pressure canner's heating system, until steam begins to escape from the valve. Once the steam hits an even stream (usually 10 minutes or so), indicating there is no more air left inside the chamber, the valve is sealed and pressure is allowed to build inside the chamber. For weighed gauge versions, the machine will automatically stop or lower the heating mechanism once the desired processing pressure and temperature is reached while the dial gauge versions will need to be monitored and adjusted accordingly. The official start time of the pressure canning cycle is when the full pressure required for the recipe is reached. After the time is complete, the pressure canner is turned off and releases pressure naturally before the jars are removed. Same as the boiling water canning, these jars should rest and cool 24 hours before being tested for any faulty seals and stored in a cool, dry environment for up to a year.

Using the Instant Pot for Pressure Canning

The Instant Pot Max model is still awaiting official USDA approval as a device to be used for pressure canning, but its makers have announced it as the first version to consistently maintain a 15-psi (pound per square inch) pressure and feature an internal thermometer to ensure the temperature of the inner chamber would rise above the 240°F (115°C) needed to pressure can foods safely. Without the official USDA seal of approval, we cannot state it is completely safe to pressure can with the Instant Pot Max; if you choose to do so, please be cognizant you are doing so at your own risk. It's also worth noting that even if the Instant Pot Max is approved, it is not able to pressure can higher than 4,800 feet above sea level.

To proceed with pressure canning in the Instant Pot max, add 2 cups of water to the inside chamber of the Instant Pot. Place the trivet or steamer basket into the Instant Pot and add in all the food or items that need to be pressure canned. All food items should be separated into sealed containers and standing upright to prevent spillage. Nothing except the trivet or steamer basket should be touching the base of the inside chamber or the water. Select Canning and set release valve to Venting to allow steam to escape in the first step of the canning process. The Instant Pot will start heating the water and steam will begin to build and escape from the release valve. In the same fashion as the dial gauge or weighted gauge pressure canners, let the steam vent for roughly 10 minutes or so to ensure it has pushed all the air from the inner chamber. Now carefully turn the release valve to Sealing and start the timing process for the food item you are pressure canning, depending on what recipe you have. The maximum amount of food you'll be able to pressure can in the Instant Pot Max—which only comes in a 6-quart capacity—is 4 pints (or 8 cups) in glass jars. Once the canning process is complete, let the Instant Pot release pressure naturally before carefully removing the lid and the food inside.

Pressure canned food should be cooled at room temperature for 24 hours before testing the seal of each lid to ensure it has properly closed in. If you are using mason jars, you should be able to remove the metal rings and easily pick up the jar without the lid coming loose. The metal lids should also not flex in either direction when pressed after canning. Properly canned items can then be stored at room temperature for up to a year. If the seal is not complete, you can either re-process the faulty jars in a jar with the same process, or refrigerate and assume a shelf life similar to pasteurization (see page 83).

Pressure Canning: Common Questions and Troubleshooting

Why pressure can instead of boiling water canning?
Pressure canning is needed for low-acid foods that do not naturally contain the compounds that prevent the growth of the *Clostridium botulinum* bacteria. Low-acid foods are classified as those over the pH level of 4.6. Even if you do not have a pH measure, it's safe to assume all vegetables, meat, fish, and dairy products must be pressure canned.

I made tomato sauce. How should I can it?
The best way to determine acidity of your tomato sauce is with a pH measure, but if you don't not have one, it is safer to pressure can.

At how many pounds of pressure should I pressure can?
This depends on your altitude and the recipe you are canning. Please refer to your recipe first as the basic guide, then adjust that pressure level and temperature based on your altitude.

Is it safe to use the Instant Pot for pressure canning?
None of the Instant Pot models except Max offer pressure canning, and it is *not* safe to pressure can in any of them. The Instant Pot Max offers pressure canning, so you can do it, but does not officially have the USDA seal of approval for home pressure canning.

Why do I need to let the steam vent from my pressure canner for so long?
Letting the steam vent for a solid 10 or so minutes is important because it ensures there is no air left inside of the inner chamber. The existence of air changes the pressure buildup and causes the temperature inside the inner chamber not to reach the necessary temperature for pressure canning.

STORAGE, CLEANING, TRANSPORTATION, AND OTHER CONSIDERATIONS

The Instant Pot is a fantastic tool that will likely last your household for many years. In order to prolong its working life to the longest possible, it's important to keep it clean and stored properly in your home. This chapter will offer guidance on the best ways to keep your Instant Pot as fresh as its first day with best practices. It also contains an overview on some essential Instant Pot accessories you may be interested in obtaining to use for your Instant Pot.

Storage

It's best to store the Instant Pot in a cool, dry location free from any loose debris, grease, or dust. The best method to store the Instant Pot's various pieces is to place the inner chamber inside the exterior, unplug the electrical cord and place it, the trivet, and spoon inside the inner chamber. Finally, place the lid on the Instant Pot properly and you have a self-contained unit that will be clean and ready for its next use!

If you don't anticipate using the Instant Pot for a while, you can also purchase an Instant Pot storage bag, which is a padded cylindrical bag that you can place the Instant Pot in for longer periods of time (or when you are traveling).

If you have multiple Instant Pot accessories (see more on that on page 110), it's a good idea to store them all close to each other for easy access. Things like extra inner chambers, extra gaskets, glass lids, steaming racks and trivets, or pot-in-pot accessories can be grouped into one or several clearly labeled bins for future use.

Cleaning

Cleaning the Instant Pot is fairly straightforward: the inner chamber and lid both can go through the dishwasher or be washed by hand after it has cooled down. The condensation cup should be removed after each use and cleaned, as well. The exterior of the appliance should be regularly wiped down with disinfectant cleaning wipes, especially at the top area where the lid locks, as that tends to build up debris over time. The electrical cord should be wiped down and kept clean, as well, and the trivet rinsed after each use and washed regularly.

If you typically use Natural Pressure Release, the lid should be fairly clean but still could use a deep clean every month or so. In order to do so, first remove the steam release handle to check for any small food particles and, if found, remove and clean with soapy water and rinse with hot water. Next, remove the anti-block shield and wipe clean the attached steam valve. This is especially important for those who frequently use the Quick Pressure Release function. Do not remove the steam valve, as that threatens the integrity of the valve. Finally, remove the float valve and clean thoroughly to ensure it is able to move easily as pressure builds.

Despite frequent cleaning, you may notice the Instant Pot begins to build up a smell inside. This is mostly due to the smells absorbed by the silicone gasket (or sealing ring). You can order additional sealing rings to swap it out—typically a good idea for every six months to a year—or you can regularly steam clean the sealing ring using water, white vinegar, and lemon. Place a 1:1 ratio of water to white vinegar in the Instant Pot, in addition to a lemon cut into wedges, and set it to Pressure Steam at High Pressure for 2 minutes with the release valve set to Sealing. Let the Instant Pot decrease pressure naturally, then carefully remove the lid to air-dry and dump the contents of the inner chamber.

Transportation

The Instant Pot is a great appliance to use when traveling, especially where there is limited space or electrical outlets. To take your Instant Pot with you on future trips, make sure you have a proper storage item that can hold the weight of your model, which can vary significantly depending on its size and model. There are snug storage bags that are cylindrical and hold the Instant Pot well, or box-shaped bags—the main thing to look for is that these storage bags have some sort of reinforcement to hold heavy items.

Some other tips for those traveling with the Instant Pot is to bring along necessary accessories, such as the trivet or steaming rack, as well as an extra sealing ring in case of emergency. Other tools such as spatulas, tongs, kitchen towels or an oven mitt, an extension cord, storage containers for food, and cleaning supplies are also very useful. Finally, a clever way to use the Instant Pot on long trips where food may be sitting in the cooler for an extended time is to freeze them in round containers, then quickly reheat or cook in the Instant Pot upon arrival at the destination. This helps ensure food doesn't spoil on the journey and keeps the cooler cold for other perishable items that cannot be frozen!

Instant Pot Accessories

Ceramic Insert

The Instant Pot comes with a stainless steel inner chamber that is machine-washable and easy to clean. However, you may notice it has a slight divot at the center where the bottom caves upward to allow space for the heating mechanism at the base of the Instant Pot. For those who frequently use the Instant Pot for functions such as searing, some opt to use the ceramic insert instead of the stainless steel inner chamber as it is flatter at the base— and also even easier to clean. This ceramic insert will not impact the cooking process in any other way. Make sure to purchase the proper size insert for your Instant Pot model.

Steaming Basket

There are many brands of steaming baskets that fit inside

the Instant Pot. This is a great accessory for those who frequently steam foods that don't fit well on top of the Instant Pot's included trivet—typically smaller food items that tend to fall through the trivet's bars. When choosing a steamer basket, opt for one that is tall and wide, efficiently giving you the most space to hold your food, as well as a silicone-covered handle(s) to quickly remove the basket from the Instant Pot after the Steam cycle is complete. Some prefer FDA-approved silicone steam baskets over food-grade stainless steel, but both work equally well—just make sure any silicone steam baskets are BPA free.

Glass Lid

The glass lid accessory is meant to help the Instant Pot mimic a traditional slow cooker and steamer by allowing small amounts of steam to escape during the cook process (see page 52). There are various brands available—when purchasing, make sure the glass lid is "tempered glass" so it can withstand necessary cooking temperatures.

Immersion Circulator

The Instant Pot branded immersion circulator—the Accu Slim Sous Vide Immersion Circulator—is a separate accessory that can be used with both the Instant Pot's inner chamber or another large vessel to create a heated water bath for sous vide cooking. The Immersion Circulator clamps to the inner chamber, either left inside or removed to the outside of the Instant Pot, and evenly circulates the water inside to the desired temperature for the food being cooked. It is not specifically different from other immersion circulators of its price range except that it works easily with the Instant Pot's physical interface—but doesn't require any functions of the Instant Pot to work. If desired, you can also use a different brand of immersion circulator with your Instant Pot's inner chamber, but may have some difficulty ensuring it secures properly to the chamber when it is still inside the Instant Pot.

Insert Pans with Sling

There are two types of insert pans for the Instant Pot: perforated and unperforated. The perforated versions are meant for steaming and certain types of baking, the other meant for cooking using the pot-in-pot method and reheating foods. The biggest advantage of using insert pans instead of a steamer basket is that they stack easily within the Instant Pot, allowing you to cook multiple things at once (as long as they are at the same time/temperature setting). Food items cooked or reheated in the insert pans can also be served in them, which helps minimize cleanup. Make sure to look for food-grade stainless steel insert pans, preferably with a silicone-covered handle(s) for easy removal from the Instant Pot.

Egg Rack

For those who love to cook eggs en masse in the Instant Pot, the egg steamer rack is a very helpful tool that lets you stack multiple layers of eggs safely in the Instant Pot. Each egg sits in a nicely indented trivet that can be placed directly into the Instant Pot, so there is no chance of it moving during the cook process. Make sure to look for racks made of food-grade stainless steel, preferably with a silicone-covered handle(s) for easy removal from the Instant Pot or with separate removal tongs.

Silicone Molds

There are many types of silicone molds for use in the Instant Pot, the most popular being the Egg Bites mold, which makes egg bites akin to those served by Starbucks. Other silicone mold shapes include specialty ones for small cakes. Select which silicone mold best suits your cooking needs but make sure to look for silicone that is BPA free.

Springform Pan

Springform pans can be used in both the Instant Pot and in regular ovens to bake various types of cakes, typically those that rise dramatically (e.g., sponge cakes). Make sure to select a leak-proof springform pan that is nonstick, has a removable bottom, and fits appropriately in your Instant Pot model and size.

ABOUT THE AUTHOR

J enny Dorsey is a professional chef, author, and artist living in New York City. She has written several books, including *Air Frying for Everyone, One Pot Meals, Kodawari by Omakase Room, Joie de Vivre by Boucherie,* and the upcoming tentatively titled *Healthy Cocktails to Shake Up Happy Hou*r (in collaboration with her mixologist husband). Jenny leads a nonprofit culinary production studio named Studio ATAO, hosts the *Why Food?* podcast on Heritage Radio Network, and runs her own consulting business. She has been profiled in outlets such as Food Network, Oxygen TV, *Eater, Food & Wine, Business Insider,* NowThis, *Bustle,* Huffington Post, and others. Jenny's writing has appeared in outlets such as VICE Munchies, Tasting Table, Narratively, Michelin Guide USA, Girlboss, TechCrunch, and more. Her full biography can be found on her website http://jennydorsey.co.

CONVERSION CHART

METRIC AND IMPERIAL CONVERSIONS
(These conversions are rounded for convenience)

Ingredient	Cups/Tablespoons/ Teaspoons	Ounces	Grams/Milliliters
Butter	1 cup/ 16 tablespoons/ 2 sticks	8 ounces	230 grams
Cheese, shredded	1 cup	4 ounces	110 grams
Cornstarch	1 tablespoon	0.3 ounce	8 grams
Cream cheese	1 tablespoon	0.5 ounce	14.5 grams
Flour, all-purpose	1 cup/1 tablespoon	4.5 ounces/0.3 ounce	125 grams/8 grams
Flour, whole wheat	1 cup	4 ounces	120 grams
Fruit, dried	1 cup	4 ounces	120 grams
Fruits or veggies, chopped	1 cup	5 to 7 ounces	145 to 200 grams
Fruits or veggies, puréed	1 cup	8.5 ounces	245 grams
Honey, maple syrup, or corn syrup	1 tablespoon	0.75 ounce	20 grams
Liquids: cream, milk, water, or juice	1 cup	8 fluid ounces	240 milliliters
Oats	1 cup	5.5 ounces	150 grams
Salt	1 teaspoon	0.2 ounces	6 grams
Spices: cinnamon, cloves, ginger, or nutmeg (ground)	1 teaspoon	0.2 ounce	5 milliliters
Sugar, brown, firmly packed	1 cup	7 ounces	200 grams
Sugar, white	1 cup/1 tablespoon	7 ounces/0.5 ounce	200 grams/12.5 grams
Vanilla extract	1 teaspoon	0.2 ounce	4 grams

INDEX

NOTES

....

....

....

....

....

....

....

....

....

....

....

....

....

....

....

NOTES

....

....

....

....

....

....

....

....

....

....

....

....

....

....

....

NOTES

....

....

....

....

....

....

....

....

....

....

....

....

....

....

....

....

NOTES

NOTES

....

....

....

....

....

....

....

....

....

....

....

....

....

....

....

....

NOTES

....

....

....

....

....

....

....

....

....

....

....

....

....

....

....

NOTES

NOTES

NOTES

....

....

....

....

....

....

....

....

....

....

....

....

....

....

....

NOTES

NOTES

....
....
....
....
....
....
....
....
....
....
....
....
....
....
....